Ad Nauseam

How Advertising and Public Relations Changed Everything

Jeff Koob

AD NAUSEAM
HOW ADVERTISING AND PUBLIC RELATIONS CHANGED EVERYTHING

iUniverse books may be ordered through booksellers or by contacting:

iUniverse
1663 Liberty Drive
Bloomington, IN 47403
www.iuniverse.com
1-800-Authors (1-800-288-4677)

ISBN: 978-1-4917-5891-5 (sc)
ISBN: 978-1-4917-5890-8 (e)

Library of Congress Control Number: 2015900818

Print information available on the last page.

iUniverse rev. date: 03/26/2015

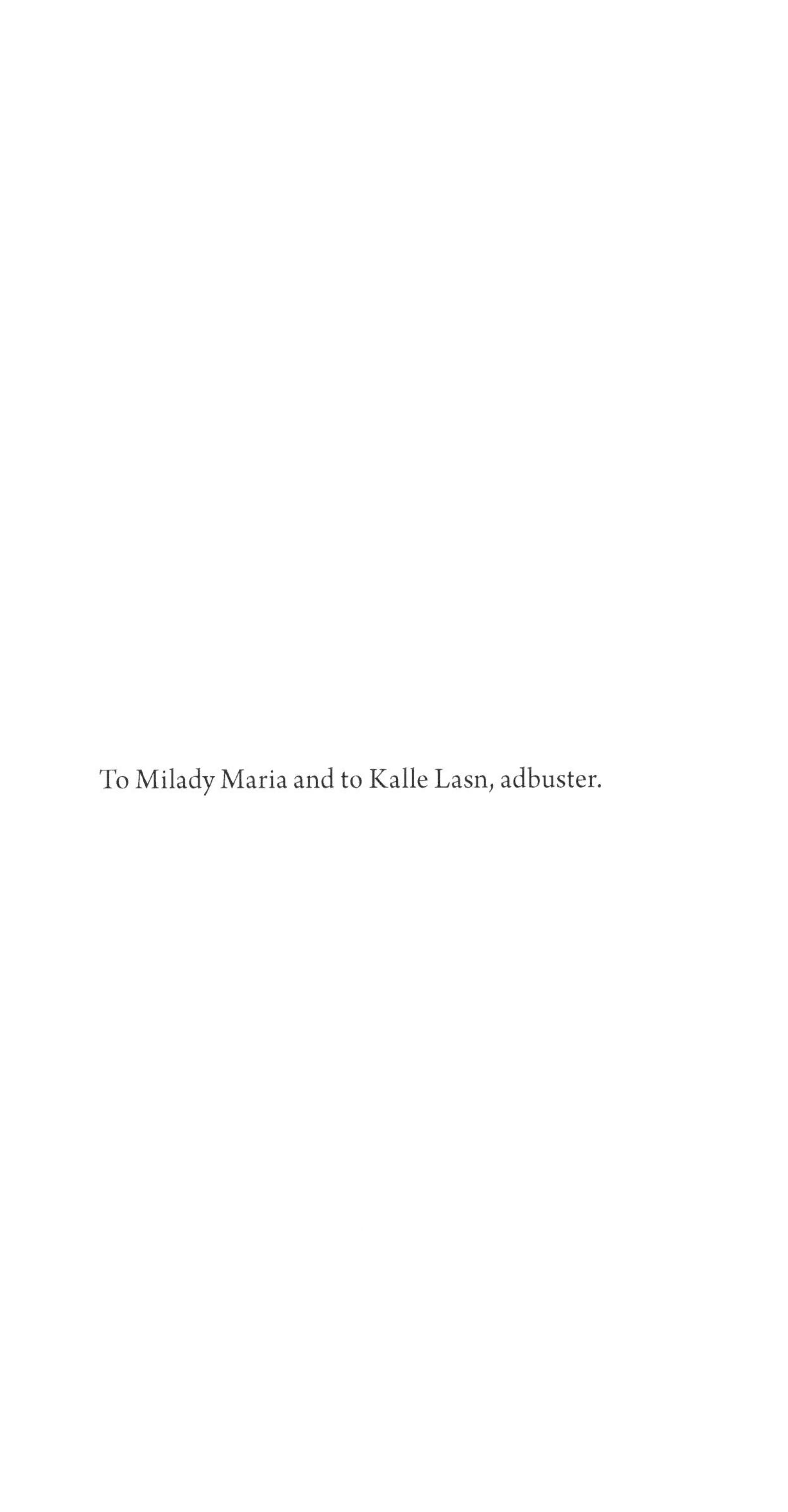

To Milady Maria and to Kalle Lasn, adbuster.

Acknowledgments

I gratefully acknowledge the patience and help of my wife and first editor, Maria Madeo, and my mother and lifelong grammar coach, Mary Koob. I'd also like to thank my brother Lindsay, my sister Laurie Britton, Dennis Adams, Martha Martin, Michael R. Wingate, and the late, great Don Weathington, who read an early draft of this book and encouraged me to finish it and get it published.

Contents

Introduction

I've been a student and a critic of advertising throughout my adult life and bring to this book the dual perspectives of having a bachelor's degree in English and a master's in psychology. I am a psychologist with more than thirty-five years of clinical practice experience. I spent more than nine years in foreign countries—four in Austria, three in Germany, and two in Jamaica—and have some perspective on cultural norms in regard to advertising practices. As you may infer from my college degrees, two of my major areas of interest are language and communication specifically and human behavior in general.

I am not against advertising. I am against its pervasiveness in our society and culture, the way it pollutes the mental environment and shapes mass behavior in negative ways. I leave it to someone else to extol the benefits that advertising has given to our culture. From my point of view, the most successful mass exploitation of the science of psychology has been in the fields of advertising and public relations. It hasn't been pretty. Kalle Lasn (1999, 19), publisher of *Adbusters* magazine, put it this way: "Corporate advertising ... is the largest single psychological project ever undertaken by the human race. Yet for all of that, its impact on us remains unknown and largely ignored."

Advertising is inescapable, and we live in a thoroughly propagandized society. The average citizen/consumer is pitched to hundreds of times a day. Why? Because it works. Commercial advertisers want to persuade you that you need their products or services, whether or not they're necessary or good for you.

Ads often promote the consumption of useless or unhealthy things and sometimes encourage people to live beyond their means. They normalize superficiality, conformity, and a mania for endless acquisition, suggesting that we need to own the biggest, the latest, the fastest, and the coolest commodities. They promulgate greed, envy, and fear as motivating emotions. Many ads employ the imperative voice—"you should ... must ... need to ..."—to tell us what we need or what to do. Manufacturers of nearly identical products spend millions of dollars to convince us that their versions are somehow superior.

At its best, advertising provides consumers with useful and accurate information about goods and services and issues. Publications such as the Yellow Pages have long served as useful guides for consumers. At its worst, advertising uses rhetorical devices, carefully crafted verbal and visual metaphors, and the psychological techniques of propaganda and behavior modification to shape opinions without regard to facts and to influence actions, often in unhealthy ways.

The intent to persuade doesn't make something propaganda, if the means of persuasion are logic and facts. It's the use of deceptive and manipulative tactics, which will be specified later, that distinguishes propaganda from information. My formal definition of propaganda is "the systematic and deliberate use of deceptive or manipulative communication techniques in the mass media to influence public attitudes, beliefs, and behaviors." A simpler formulation is "media presentations and campaigns that employ techniques of deception and subconscious influence."

Advertising has become so ubiquitous that it influences every aspect of our lives: medicine, the law, economics, diet, child rearing, information and entertainment sources, spiritual life, political affiliations, lifestyle choices, and voting patterns as well as the clothes we wear and the goods and services we purchase. It is no more intrinsically good or evil than fire. But like fire, it can have a creative or a destructive effect, depending on how it's used and to what end it is employed.

This book includes two appendices. The first is my previously unpublished essay, "On Commodities," which some readers may want to read first. You'll see some of the seeds of *Ad Nauseam* in that essay, which I wrote years ago. The second appendix started with a list I kept over many years, which tracked claims made by TV advertisers. "100 Things You Learn on TV" provides examples of absurd or silly commercial messages and the convoluted, illogical formulations that are presented as true.

Propaganda Society

We live in a society so saturated by propaganda that its mechanisms and influence are invisible to most people, which is a hallmark of its success. It is an integral part of the sea of information/entertainment in which we all swim. (Do fish realize that they're wet?) Propaganda—which includes some advertising, public relations, and political campaigns—is thriving in the industrialized world.

US advertising is at least a $130-billion-a-year industry. Estimates about how many commercial messages the average American is exposed to on a daily basis vary widely, from 250 on the conservative end to as high as one thousand or more. Among the significant variables are whether you live in an urban or rural environment and how much commercial media you consume, but it's safe to say that the average is somewhere in the hundreds. According to Pratkanis and Aronson (2001, 14), "The average American will see or hear more than seven million advertisements in his or her lifetime." As Lasn (1999, 11) explains, "Identical images flow into our brain, homogenizing our perspectives, knowledge, tastes and desires."

What passes for truth-in-advertising laws are a sham and a farce, in my opinion, and much of the time advertisers are more interested in perception than facts. Many ads are unburdened by anything resembling truth. In the past, medical doctors couldn't endorse drugs or medical products, and lawyers couldn't advertise their services on TV. There were good reasons for these restrictions, but those days are gone, to the detriment of not only those professions but the public welfare.

Competing medical and legal services are marketed like cornflakes. In what I call the "arms race effect," lawyers, doctors, and politicians start to advertise on TV, and their competitors have to advertise to keep up. TV ads portray hospitals and other care facilities as resorts, and their advertising costs are added to patients' bills.

Due to the absence of effective regulation, we have print ads for pills that are "guaranteed" to help you shed unwanted pounds or reverse the effects of aging. Although most of the drug and alcohol treatment community agrees that there is no cure for addiction, a cure is just what certain TV ads for substance-abuse treatment promise. And if you're a lonely Christian single looking for a mate, a TV spot promises to find "God's match for you." Apparently even God sometimes needs help from the advertising industry.

The progressive influence of sophisticated advertising and public relations industries in the twentieth century was amplified by the successive availability of new mass communication technologies. Using the classic techniques of propaganda and other manipulative tactics, the advertising and public relations industries have intentionally and systematically blurred the line between reality and fiction. And in the current system of mass information dissemination, perception often trumps facts. It's not so much what people know as what they think they know that sells products and wins elections. This calculated trend of engineered consent endangers democracy.

If you asked most Americans about propaganda, they'd say it is something that happens elsewhere. We're so steeped in propaganda techniques that most of us don't notice them in advertising and public relations campaigns. I'm convinced that most Americans would deny the influence of propaganda in their own lives. It's easy to see propaganda as it is used in totalitarian states that control the popular media, because it comes from a centralized source. It takes a different shape in capitalist democracies because it's diversified, with a variety of sources and competing messages. But the techniques are the same.

Propaganda versus Information

What differentiates propaganda from information? The most basic difference is that the goal of propaganda is not to inform but to influence. Ad campaigns tout more product for less money but never let the consumer know that product size or quality has diminished relative to the cost. That would be information.

Propagandists use emotion and unfounded assertions rather than logic and fact, selecting emotionally loaded words and images to create a desired feeling, or combining facts and half-truths—or outright lies—with emotional triggers. They use rhetorical tricks and the psychological behavior-modification techniques of classical and operant conditioning to manipulate mass behavior. Much of the commercial advertising that bombards us daily is propaganda, as is almost all political advertising these days.

In the political arena, propaganda depicts the very wealthy as "job creators" rather than "robber barons." The truth runs deeper than such simplistic labels. Speculation about a candidate's motives is a fair journalistic tactic (e.g., "Does Obama have a socialist agenda?"). Propaganda is attributing motives without proof (e.g., "Obama has a secret socialist agenda"). In cognitive psychology, the latter assertion would be classified as a thinking error called mindreading: "I know what he's thinking, why he did that." Behavior can be observed and described in a way that motives can't.

It has been said that Gutenberg "invented" public opinion with the innovation of movable type. Since the concept of the public took hold, clever people have endeavored to influence its opinions—some with facts and others with propaganda—utilizing the available mass communication technologies, starting with pamphlets and posters. Radio, newsreels, and movies were the technologies used by both the Axis and the Allied powers during World War II to convince the masses to support their respective war efforts.

Lessons learned about the effectiveness of propaganda during the world wars were not lost on twentieth-century advertising and public relations industries. When television came along, it was clear from the start that—at least in the United States—commercial sponsorship would be its engine. Some people believe that the primary function of the mass media is merchandising. Rush Limbaugh put it this way: "A turning point in my career came when I realized that the sole purpose for all of us in radio is to sell advertising" (Viguerie 2004, 179).

The dynamic combination of instant audiovisual communication and psychotechnologies, such as classical and operant conditioning, has made propaganda all the more effective in influencing opinion and behavior on a grand scale. As a psychologist, it disturbs me greatly to see that our society's primary, systematic application of the principles of psychology has been as a tool for commercial and political persuasion and for the manipulation of behavior in the service of commerce.

A propagandized society is antithetical to democracy, which depends on an educated and well-informed electorate. Again, the purpose of propaganda isn't to inform but to influence. Advertising and public relations often use persuasion techniques in the guise of offering information. While most journalists are held to a standard of objectivity and factual reporting, advertisers and public relations professionals are under no such constraints. Their purpose is to make you *feel* a certain way about some product or service or issue, while making you think you *know* something important. Their craft is selling you a version of the truth that suits their purposes.

In the pages that follow, I'll ask you to imagine a world without advertising and then a world with "sane," ethical advertising. I'll write about the origins of our propaganda society. Next I'll briefly elaborate on what differentiates propaganda from information, and define the heuristics and communications techniques that propagandists use to influence public perceptions. I'll describe rhetorical devices, behavior modification techniques, the unconscious mind, systems theory, and situationalism. Finally, I'll explain how advertising and public relations have infiltrated every aspect of our lives and their involvement in the decline of democracy, public health, the mental environment, and the ecological health of the biosphere.

Sane Advertising

In a world without advertising, all the signs would be traffic related or "official."

If you came to a place you'd never been before, you'd have to rely on word of mouth or a municipal directory to find out where to obtain goods and services. Ideally, the information in the directory would be objective; the personal recommendations, of course, would be subjective. There would be no classified ads or commercial signs, except possibly small generic ones, like HOTEL or FOOD. There would be no commercials on radio or TV, which would be underwritten by subscription fees. Since advertising is a mainstay of marketing, innovative competition no longer would be stimulated. Fashion would dry up, to be replaced by generic trends and subculture uniforms. Information on bargains would be hard to come by. Celebrities couldn't profit from their fame by endorsing products. Political advertising would be fact based, presenting the candidate's merits and proposals and not the opponent's alleged shortcomings. In manufacturing, the high standard would be average. Radio and TV programming wouldn't be ratings driven.

I'm not suggesting that all the things I've listed in the thought experiment above are desirable. I've interspersed the good with the bad, as I see it, and I leave it to you to decide which is which. I'm just inviting you to imagine how different things would be in a world without any advertising or PR.

Now imagine a world with sane, ethical advertising. In such a world people could trust ads as accurate and factual. Signs advertising goods and service would be modest in size, with no ongoing competition for bigger and bigger signs. Truth-in-advertising laws would have teeth: nobody would be allowed to claim the "cure" for something or the "best" service or the "lowest cost" unless those claims were backed up with objective proof. Children wouldn't be targeted with ads for unhealthy products, and advertising for harmful things like alcohol and tobacco would be regulated or banned in the media.

Advertising on television would be shown in blocks between programs, and shows wouldn't be cut up into standard-length, *N*-minute segments to allow for messages from the sponsors. Having advertising that wasn't tied to specific shows would end the endless ratings war that gives us programming aimed at the lowest common denominator, resulting in a higher quality of programming. (I'll expand on this proposition later.)

We would no longer have to deal with the mental pollution of constant bombardment by commercial messages: wasteful paper flyers and pamphlets in the mail and in newspapers; periodicals that have almost as much advertising as content; huge billboards and other advertising signage; voices blaring from PA systems in malls; robocalls; broadcast media that fill our heads with slogans, jingles, and hollow promises; product placement in movies; spam e-mail; websites and phone apps that make you view advertising before you can access content. In this ideal world, advertising would be grounded in information and assistance rather than in propaganda and behavior-modification techniques.

Love or Fear?

Advertising is pervasive *because* it influences buying habits. Effective advertising generates revenue, whether you're selling vitamins or cigarettes. There's a saying in the ad industry, "If you can't win them with love, win them with fear." You can sell cookies by saying that they're baked by cute elves. You can sell mouthwash by labeling bad breath as serious-sounding halitosis and suggesting that people who have it don't get laid or promoted.

The term halitosis was popularized in a 1920s ad campaign for Listerine. With the headline "Often a Bridesmaid but Never a Bride," the ad stated:

> Edna's case was really a pathetic one. Like every woman, her primary ambition was to marry ... As her birthdays crept gradually toward that tragic thirty mark, marriage seemed farther from her life than ever. She was often a bridesmaid but never a bride ... That's the insidious thing about halitosis (unpleasant breath). You, yourself, rarely know when you have it. And even your closest friends won't tell you.

The ad implies that Edna's dismal matrimonial prospects are due solely to her foul breath and then provides a remedy for those who identify with her plight. The implication is, since even your best friends won't tell you your breath stinks, you should use Listerine daily. Decades later in a TV ad, actress Gail Storm recommended using Listerine every time people brushed their teeth, to "finish the job."

Public Relations Spin Cycle

Not all public relations work is propaganda. Some PR campaigns stick to the facts and provide relevant information about their clients and about circumstances relevant to their clients' interests. Many campaigns that were clearly in the public interest have not resorted to manipulative techniques to get out their messages.

Many PR professionals consider themselves to be social science specialists, and some of the techniques they use are referred to as "applied social science." Techniques include denial and minimizing; assertion is the propaganda term for stating an opinion as a fact. Other techniques are distortion, distraction, and reframing (manipulating the context).

One means of reframing used by public relations consultants is creative naming. States with laws against mandatory union membership are called "right-to-work" states. People who oppose abortion are called "pro-life," and those who want abortion to remain legal are dubbed "pro-choice." Any attempt to provide universal health insurance is labeled "socialized medicine." Immense stinking pits of excrement on hog farms are called "lagoons." Corporations don't engage in the mass firing of employees anymore; they "downsize." There is such a thing, we are told, as "clean coal."

Public relations professionals are frequently in the business of denying facts or spinning them so that they no longer resemble the truth. Here's my take on the stages of a typical PR campaign. There have been successive revelations that Sam Smith, CEO of Squeaky Klean Corp., knowingly hired Joe Shoddy to dispose of hazardous chemicals cheaply and illegally. As new evidence continues to be discovered, the successive PR messages are as follows:

1. No hazardous chemicals from Squeaky Klean Corp. were ever dumped in the river.
2. If, in fact, any chemicals from Squeaky Klean Corp. were dumped in the river, company officials didn't know anything about it.
3. Joe Shoddy's company provided the lowest bid to dispose of hazardous chemicals, but we assumed that he'd do the job responsibly. We may have known about some past violations, but Squeaky Klean Corp. was not aware of the extent of Shoddy's illegal dumping when the contract was signed.
4. Sam Smith wasn't aware that the Squeaky Klean board had accepted the bid of a contractor with a long history of illegal dumping of toxic chemicals. It was a corporate decision.
5. While Sam Smith is Joe Shoddy's father-in-law, there were no improprieties, and no laws were broken.
6. If Sam Smith unknowingly broke any laws, it is because he has bipolar disorder.

Public relations is part of the fabric of modern life, and every major corporation, organization, and enterprise has a PR component, which serves as its "voice." PR goes by many names in both the private and public sectors, including community relations, public information, publicity, media relations, communications consultancy, public affairs, campaign management, and political consultancy. Sometimes PR professionals and advertising copy writers try to pass for reporters, although they serve a fundamentally different function—to persuade in the guise of providing objective information.

At their best, public relations campaigns influence people to do good things like stop littering ("Keep America Beautiful") and prevent forest fires (Smokey the Bear's "Only you can prevent forest fires!"). At their worst, they mislead people or create smoke screens for corporate misadventures, often using the tricks and techniques of propaganda.

How Propaganda Works

In his 1922 book *Public Opinion,* Walter Lippmann wrote about the herd mentality and argued that it is necessary in a democracy for a power elite to "manufacture consent," a term echoed in later writings by Edward Bernays and Noam Chomsky. Lippmann (1922, 158) contended that because of psychological research and "the modern means of communication, the practice of democracy has turned a corner. A revolution is taking place, infinitely more significant than any shift in economic power." He suggested that it was necessary for public opinion to be managed by professionals skilled in the "art of persuasion." He used the term "pictures in our heads" to describe how the popular media influences our thinking (Lippmann 1922, 3).

The Father of Public Relations and the Invisible Government

The self-appointed "father of public relations," Edward Bernays—a nephew and confidante of Sigmund Freud—shared Lippmann's conviction that in a democracy, the herd couldn't be relied upon to govern itself, and skilled technicians were needed to bring order to chaos. "Modern propaganda," he wrote in his book *Propaganda,* "is a consistent, enduring effort to create or shape events to influence the relations of the public to an enterprise, idea or group ... It was, of course, the astounding success of propaganda during the war that opened the eyes of the intelligent few ... to the possibilities of regimenting the public mind" (Bernays 1928, 52, 54). But since the word *propaganda* had gotten a bad reputation in wartime, he gave it a new name and a new face: *public relations.*

Edward Bernays learned his craft working for the US Committee on Public Information, otherwise known as the Creel Committee. George Creel had been appointed by President Woodrow Wilson to form a committee whose purpose was to influence public opinion in favor of American participation in World War I. Creel later wrote a book, *How We Advertised America,* in which he hyperbolically claimed that the committee had "carried the Gospel of Americanism to Every Corner of the Globe" (Lippmann 1922, 30). He used the term *advertised* instead of *propagandized* in his title, because of the negative connotations the latter term had acquired. In *Mein Kampf,* Hitler expressed his admiration for the British and American propaganda campaigns of WWI, acknowledging that he'd learned a lot from them.

In his book, Bernays promoted both propaganda and himself. He proposed a new profession: the public relations counsel (in the sense of legal counsel). "The modern propagandist," he wrote, "... sets to work to create circumstances which will modify [the] custom ... By playing on an old cliché, or manipulating a new one, the propagandist can sometimes swing a whole mass of group emotions" (Bernays

1928, 74, 77). *Propaganda* wasn't just an essay on the benefits of its subject, it was a guidebook for would-be practitioners of the craft.

Central to the success of this technology of influence is its invisibility: most people affected by it don't see themselves as propagandized. "Is it not possible to control and regiment the masses according to our will without their knowing about it?" Bernays asked and asserted that it was: "Propaganda is the executive arm of the invisible government" (1928, 48, 71). He wrote:

> The conscious and intelligent manipulation of the organized habits and opinions of the masses is an important element in democratic society. Those who manipulate this unseen mechanism of society constitute an invisible government which is the true ruling power of our country. We are governed, our minds are molded, our tastes formed, our ideas suggested, largely by men we have never heard of. (Bernays 1928, 37)

Bernays (1928, 38) explained that we are being covertly governed by a "relatively small number of persons ... who understand the mental processes and social patterns of the masses. It is they who pull the wires which control the public mind, who harness old social forces and contrive new ways to bind and guide the world." His rationalization for rule by an invisible government was that "we have voluntarily agreed" to it (Bernays 1928, 38). He predicted that "propaganda will never die out" and said that its use is "growing as its efficiency in gaining public support is recognized" (Bernays 1928, 168). Believing in the collective wisdom of a benign intellectual elite over the will of the masses, he substituted propaganda for information in his equation for democracy and provided a blueprint for its implementation.

Edward Bernays had a long and successful career in the new profession he'd introduced and defined. He described the linking of products and ideas to unconscious desires, how the public could be made to want things that they didn't need. He represented hundreds of clients and made a lot of money molding public opinion. In the late 1920s, he used his principles of social science to change women's attitudes about cigarette smoking—destigmatizing it and associating it with power, liberation, and weight control. He pushed the notion that smoking soothes the throat and claimed that a "toasting process" had removed the irritants from cigarettes.

He has been given or took credit for such things as establishing bacon and eggs as the all-American breakfast, promoting beer as a "beverage of moderation" compared to distilled spirits, abbreviating multiple sclerosis to MS in the public mind, and changing mental hygiene to mental health. He advised public relations counsels to employ the methods of the social scientist, carefully studying both the client and the market (or the public) before formulating strategy and giving advice.

Bernays has some rivals in his claim to be the father of public relations, but he wrote the book on what he called "crystallizing public opinion." (It was the title of his first book, written in 1923.) Using "appeals of indirection" and his knowledge of his famous uncle's theories, Bernays often aimed at the gut more than the brain in attempting to shape mass behavior. He was arguably one of the preeminent professional opinion molders of the twentieth century. His rich legacy continues to influence propaganda and public relations.

Ivy Ledbetter Lee was one of Bernays's principle competitors. Ivy Lee and Associates was one of the first international public relations firms and represented German chemical giant I. G. Farben early in the Nazi era. Another influential public relations pioneer, Daniel Edelman, got his start analyzing propaganda during World War II. Edelman was assigned to a "psychological warfare" unit to study German propaganda. He used what he learned about influencing mass behavior to build a major international public relations empire, eventually employing more than four thousand employees in sixty-six countries.

The Father of Behaviorism

J. B Watson, the "father of behaviorism," also applied his scientific discipline—psychology—to campaigns of mass persuasion. In the first half of the twentieth century, behaviorism was the preeminent school of psychology after Freudian theory. It describes human behavior in terms of how we learn, which is the same way other sentient species learn, by stimulus and response. Behaviors that are positively reinforced tend to be repeated, and behavior can be shaped using the principles of systematic reinforcement.

After losing his position on the faculty of Johns Hopkins University due to a scandal involving an affair with a graduate assistant, Watson went to work for the J. Walter Thompson advertising agency, one of the biggest in New York City. He made a lot more money promoting such products as Ponds

Cold Cream and Maxwell House Coffee than he'd made in academia. In the latter ad campaign, he promoted the institution of the "coffee break." He believed in using market research to target consumers and that effective advertising should appeal to basic emotions—love, fear, anger—and left his mark as a psychotechnician on the effective mass manipulation of behavior.

The Birth of Political Consultancy

An inevitable offshoot of the PR industry was political consultancy, and the preeminent pioneers of political spin were Clem Whitaker and Leone Baxter, whose business, Campaigns Inc., was called "the Lie Factory" by novelist and would-be governor of California Upton Sinclair (Lepore 2012, 50). Campaigns Inc. was founded in 1933; according to Jill Lepore (2012, 54), "No single development has altered the workings of American democracy in the last century so much as political consulting, an industry unknown before Campaigns Inc." Among the tactics employed against Sinclair by Campaigns, Inc. was to send articles about him to periodicals and attribute quotes from characters in his novels to Sinclair, as if those words reflected his personal beliefs.

Political consultancy became indispensable to the political process, with its polling, market research, advertising, and public relations components. Among Whitaker and Baxter's recommendations for marketing candidates was to avoid detailed explanations where possible but instead to simplify and repeat the message. According to Whitaker, "The more you have to explain, the more difficult it is to win support" (Lepore 2012, 55). Politicians don't say much in public these days without running their comments by, or getting them from, their political advisors.

In 1945 President Truman tried to get health care recognized as a public responsibility. Whitaker and Baxter mounted a campaign for the American Medical Association (AMA) that popularized the term "socialized medicine." Truman was so angry at this attempt to defeat his national health insurance program, he told the press that "nothing in this bill came anywhere closer to socialism than the payments the AMA makes to the advertising firm of Whitaker and Baxter to misrepresent my health program" (Lepore 2012, 58). The term *socialized medicine* has proven to have legs and is still used by Republican propagandists to discredit the Affordable Care Act.

By the mid-1950s, political consultancy had become a fixture in national politics, and things have never been the same. Adlai Stevenson observed, "The idea that you can merchandise candidates for high office like breakfast cereal ... is the ultimate indignity to the democratic process" (Quoteswave).

The GOPAC Memo and Beyond

Political consultancy theories and techniques continue to influence politics. Edward Bernays (1928, 120) once wondered in print "whether the politicians of the future, who are responsible for maintaining the prestige and effectiveness of their party, will not endeavor to train politicians who are at the same time propagandists." He seems to have been prescient, predicting such politicians as Newt Gingrich. Although Gingrich wasn't strictly speaking a professional political consultant, he did his part to advance the use of propaganda tactics in his 1996 GOPAC memo (Information

Clearing House), which gave potential conservative political candidates words and terms for characterizing their opponents. He wrote, "Often we search hard for words to define our opponents. Sometimes we are hesitant to use contrast. Remember that creating a difference helps you. These are powerful words that can create a clear and easily understood contrast. Apply these to your opponent, their record, proposals, and their party."

Among the words he listed were: abuse of power, anti (-flag, -family, -child, -job), betray, bizarre, cheat, coercion, corrupt, decay, destroy, devour, disgrace, failure, greed, hypocrisy, incompetent, intolerant, liberal, lie, obsolete, pathetic, punish, radical, red tape, selfish, shallow, shame, sick, stagnation, steal, taxes, traitors, unionized, waste, and welfare. Gingrich didn't apply these words to actual individuals; he provided the menu of emotionally loaded words for exploitative purposes. I find it especially revelatory of the right-wing Republican mind-set that the words *liberal, taxes, unionized,* and *welfare* appear among the other clearly pejorative nouns and adjectives that constitute most of the list.

The ability to effectively spin facts has become central to political debate. In the wake of President Obama's reelection in 2012, Republican political consultant Frank Luntz wrote an article in the January 11, 2013, issue of the *Washington Post,* "Why Republicans Should Watch Their Language." In it he identified what he called a "messaging problem" and "language errors" in the party's strategy. Instead of "smaller government," which is clearly what the Republican Party currently advocates, Luntz advised changing the wording to "more efficient and effective government." Instead of "tax reform," they should say "making the IRS code simpler, flatter, and fairer." Instead of "capping" spending, they should "control" it. Instead of "entitlement reform" or "controlling the growth of Medicare and Social Security," politicians should say they want to "save and strengthen entitlements." Instead of discussing "economic opportunity and growth," frame the dialogue as "creating a healthier and more secure economy."

Political consultancy has wrought big changes in our political system at all levels of government. Party decisions that used to be hammered out in smoke-filled rooms and on the convention floor are now made under the advisement of professional pollsters and propagandists. No serious candidate for high office would dream of mounting a campaign without first hiring the best political consultants he or she can afford.

Mass media advertising campaigns cost a lot of money, and as a result, most politicians spend significant time, day in and day out, soliciting contributions for their campaign funds. The Supreme Court's *Citizens United* ruling gave our wealthiest citizens even more political clout, as they can now underwrite even more political propaganda ads. On the November 3, 2014, broadcast of his PBS program "Moyers and Company," Bill Moyers said an estimated $4 billion had been spent on advertising during the 2014 midterm elections. That kind of spending is unprecedented and is likely to increase.

Propaganda Strategies and Advertising

The success of propaganda as a political tool hasn't escaped the advertising industry. In their book *Age of Propaganda: The Everyday Use and Abuse of Persuasion*, Anthony Pratkanis and Elliot Aronson (2001, 11) write, "Propaganda involves the dexterous use of images, slogans, and symbols that play on our prejudices and emotions." The basic principles of advertising and marketing were codified early in the twentieth century and taught in colleges and universities, they write: "Propagandists attempt to take advantage of our two basic human tendencies—to take mental shortcuts and to rationalize our behavior—by constructing various tactics that play on our prejudices and emotions ... Advertisers know all too well that we believe what we believe and buy what we buy in the service of our self-image" (Pratkanis and Aronson 2001, 32).

Pratkanis and Aronson identify four stratagems of influence: (1) *prepersuasion*: framing, setting the context; (2) *source credibility*: creating a favorable brand image; (3) *message*: focusing the target's thinking; and (4) *emotions*: activating a motivating emotion. They also examine slogans—commercial and political—and reveal that the keys to successful sloganeering are simplicity and repetition.

In *The Ten Commandments of Propaganda,* Brian Anse Patrick (2012, back cover) defines propaganda as "the scientific art of interpreting someone else's reality for them in order to benefit the propagandist. Propaganda is junk food for the mind." One of the ten commandments he identifies is disambiguation, presenting things in black-and-white terms, excluding any shades of gray. "Ambiguity," he writes, "is the enemy of propaganda" (Patrick 2012, 57).

Not all advertisements deserve the propaganda label, but many do. One of the most commonly used propaganda techniques in advertising is the presentation of opinions as facts. Another is the repetition of a simple message or slogan, over and over.

Advertising is essentially amoral, but in my opinion,

some of its manifestations are immoral. One example is advertising's ability to make unhealthy behavior seem normal and to promote the consumption of unhealthy products. Normal is neither good nor bad from a psychological point of view, although many people still view normality as a desirable state. Normal just means that a lot of people do it. What is considered normal differs from culture to culture and can change over time.

Smoking used to be considered a normal behavior for adults. Advertisers promoted it, and the tobacco industry's PR representatives minimized the health risks and denied that nicotine was addictive. The first surgeon general's report to connect smoking with major health problems came out in 1964, but the tobacco industry didn't acknowledge the link until 1999. For years they pushed the notion that filters made cigarettes safer, although there was no scientific evidence to back it up. If the tobacco industry still had its way, the Marlboro Man would remain an icon for American smokers, and there would be no warning labels on cigarette packages.

From 1953 to 1968 the public relations firm Hill and Knowlton represented the tobacco industry and tried to discredit the notion that smoking might cause lung cancer. In 1954, the firm released "A Frank Statement to Cigarette Smokers" to four hundred newspapers, and forty-three million readers, disputing reports that cigarette smoking caused lung cancer and other dangerous health conditions. The goal was to create doubt. Public relations firms representing the natural gas industry continue to use that tactic by raising doubts about risks associated with hydraulic fracturing.

Tobacco smoking is no longer considered a normal behavior in our culture. Smoking now carries a stigma, as well it should, because it is a recognized addiction and a massive public health problem. Due in part to restrictions on tobacco advertising, cigarette smoking in the United States dropped from 43 percent of adults in 1964 to 18 percent in 2013 (Morin 2014). Globally, however, tobacco remains a growth industry, and advertising continues to influence nonsmokers to take up the addictive habit. As long as they aren't held liable, many advertisers don't care if the products they promote are toxic.

In the introduction to the 2007 edition of Vance Packard's classic book on advertising, *The Hidden Persuaders* (1957, 9), Mark Crispin Miller writes, "... the modern history of America is, in large part, the history of an ever-rising flood of corporate propaganda." Packard (1957, 3) described his book as being about "the large-scale efforts being made, often with impressive success, to channel our unthinking habits, our purchasing decisions, and our thought processes by the use of insights gleaned from psychiatry and the social sciences ... many of us are being influenced and manipulated, far more than we realize, in the patterns of our everyday lives." He identified "symbol manipulation and reiteration" as mainstays of political persuasion and introduces such concepts as "triggers of action" (words and pictures), the "psychological hook," and the use of sexual imagery as "eye stoppers."

The main topic of *The Hidden Persuaders* is the rise of motivational research in marketing. Citing a 1950 article—"How Psychiatric Methods Can Be Applied to Marketing Research" by James Vicary in the marketing journal *Printers' Ink*—Packard stated that hundreds of social scientists were being hired by marketing and advertising agencies. Projective psychological tests like the Rorschach and the Thematic Apperception Test were used to identify personality types as well as methods and themes that could be used to influence people. Psychology provided marketers with information they could use to promote brand loyalty and create in consumers an emotional bond with a product.

Over the course of the twentieth century, we moved from a need-driven economy to what might be called a wish-fulfillment economy. That couldn't have happened without advertising. Now that I've examined how we came to be a propaganda society and how advertising has borrowed many of the tools of the propagandist's trade, I'll show you just what those tools are.

Tricks and Techniques

To have a thorough understanding of how information and propaganda differ fundamentally, you need to know the tricks and techniques propagandists use. There will be some degree of overlap between some of the terms that follow. For simplicity's sake, I'll use *advertisers*, but these methods also are employed by public relations representatives and political consultants.

What distinguishes the propagandist from the honest broker of information? Some earnest information brokers tell you untruths that they believe to be truths, and there's a considerable gray area between the black-and-white poles of truth versus lies. I propose that the antithesis of the propagandist is the communicator who acts in good faith, trying his or her best to be objective, and clearly separating fact from opinion.

Different standards of journalistic accountability are applied to reporters for major news organizations (excluding tabloid journalists) than to so-called pundits and bloggers.

My ideal candidates as purveyors of information are those communicators who would never knowingly present something as true without having a good reason to believe it was fact-based, a person who feels a duty to be broadly informed, objective, and truthful.

Before I get into the techniques of propaganda, however, I'll examine some of the basic building-blocks of influence: words and phrases, metaphors, and heuristics.

Words and Phrases

Some individual words clearly resonate with people more than others, because they evoke emotional responses or promote positive associations. Savvy influence peddlers like to use these words a lot, often in combination with images that complement or amplify their influence. Some popular influential nouns are happiness, satisfaction, power, control, security, excitement, love, luxury, and trust. Examples of popular influential verbs are believe, dare, win, deserve, accomplish, introducing, trust, love, and enjoy. There are numerous popular influential adjectives, including clean, new, quick, easy, best, most, fast, free, proven, improved, proud, rugged, successful, amazing, outstanding, unbeatable, powerful, and extra-strength. (I culled these words from several how-to books on writing advertising copy.)

Influential phrases can take the form of clichés, slogans, and directives in the imperative voice, such as Coke's "Open happiness!" or Nike's "Just Do It." Such phrases needn't mean anything objectively but are used to promote an emotional state or aura. Other examples are:

- low (or lower) prices

- more for your money
- and that's not all
- satisfaction guaranteed
- I'm a believer
- the more you buy, the more you save
- why settle for less?

Whether or not these phrases reflect objective reality, they can influence us.

Metaphors

A metaphor is a literary device used to describe one thing in terms of another. Similes do much the same, using "like" or "as" to couch the comparison. In his book, *I Is an Other,* James Geary (2011, 19) writes, "Nothing is as exact as an apt metaphor." He states that the tactical use of metaphor in advertising "surreptitiously infiltrates our purchasing decisions ... Successful advertisements depend almost entirely on metaphors that resonate with the target audience" (Geary 2011, 3, 59). Metaphorical thinking, he explains, influences our beliefs and behaviors in ways we're usually not consciously aware of.

Our brains work by recognizing patterns, and we often think in metaphors. Much of what we say and write is expressed in metaphors, which allow us to describe abstract things such as emotions and ideas: His heart took wing. You are my sunshine. He's a rock. Their apt use in messages directed at us can influence our daily experiences, often imperceptibly.

Metaphors can be visual, such as the cartoon image of a light bulb that signifies an idea or an aha moment, or giving someone the finger. Allstate places you in good hands. Prudential shows you the Rock of Gibraltar. Travelers gives you an umbrella. Ads for Fidelity Investments suggest the company will provide customers with a moving green path that they can follow to prosperity.

Although they aren't generally considered metaphors, I'd argue that personifying or anthropomorphizing a product is a kind of audiovisual metaphor: if this product were a person, what would it say? These techniques portray products as having human characteristics with which we can identify and give them what I call anthropomorphic agency. For example, a household cleaner can scrub for us. A nutritional supplement is like a drill sergeant in your fridge, driving out unhealthy foods. A voiceover says "Nutrition in charge!" equating the product with good nutrition. Mr. Clean is a walking metaphor, a personification of the desired outcome of housecleaning. He hates dirt.

Some ads are direct, while others use a peripheral approach to get their messages across. TV ad copywriters and graphic designers work together to combine resonant verbal and visual metaphors into powerful commercial messages that I call stealth ads: they are designed to fly beneath the radar of rational thought and objective reasoning, and deliver an influential message "invisibly."

Pavlov's dogs were systematically conditioned to salivate when they heard a bell ring. Many of us have been systematically conditioned to salivate at the sight of golden arches or the image of a deceased Kentucky colonel. Seeing images of other people eating food that we like triggers our hunger and makes us want to eat that food too. In this regard, we are very much like beagles and terriers.

Heuristics

A heuristic is a concept of a different order than words, phrases, and metaphors; heuristics are tools that are used strategically by marketers and advertisers to influence behavior on a mass scale. Heuristics are mental shortcuts we use in decision making that can be exploited by influence peddlers. When we don't have time to think things through comprehensively, or feel overwhelmed by the press of incoming information, we resort to heuristics. They include:

- *trial and error*
- *educated guess*
- *common sense* (as we individually apprehend it)
- *working backward* (from solved problem to method of solution)
- *rule of thumb* (approximation)
- *stereotyping* (if this, then that)

Then there is the *consistency* heuristic, where a person responds in a manner consistent with his self-image; the *familiarity* heuristic, where one recognizes a situation and responds just as one has before; the *scarcity* heuristic, where rare things are represented as more desirable (e.g., "this offer is limited"); the *authority* heuristic, where we believe the endorsement of an authority figure; and the *affect* heuristic, where we make a snap judgment based on a quick, affect-influenced impression. The *social consensus* heuristic uses modeling of the target behavior by attractive people to suggest that we should join the in-crowd. ("Wouldn't you like to be a Pepper too?" "Pepsi, for those who think young!") The *persuasion* heuristic explains why pitch people on radio and TV come across as confident and highly enthusiastic about the great deals they're hyping. The *price-value* heuristic works when we believe a product to be superior because it costs more.

There is considerable overlap between heuristics as defined here and propaganda techniques and other manipulations that rely on heuristic influence. For instance, the social consensus heuristic correlates to the bandwagon technique (described below).

Propaganda Tools

A propagandist isn't bound by the strictures of objectivity and reliance on facts. He or she doesn't have a primary allegiance to the public welfare, but to the company or interest group that pays for his or her services. Some propaganda is benign and serves the public welfare, as do certain public service campaigns. While the ideal purveyor of information strives to speak truthfully and objectively for the benefit of all, propagandists want to influence people to benefit the enterprise or the interest group they serve.

What follows is a list of the propagandist's tools. Many of them were identified by the Institute for Propaganda Analysis (Cole 1998, 360–61), a public interest group founded in New York in 1937. Its stated goal was "to teach people how to think rather than what to think." Others, such as pseudoinformation, were derived from my observations. The outright lie is the most basic tool of the propagandist/advertiser. Any unsubstantiated use of terms—such as "we always give you more!"; "best deal in town"; and "we do it better!"—qualifies as an outright lie. This technique—stating opinion as fact—is also known as *assertion*. The words "more" and "better" are meaningless if the phrases and sentences that contain them don't specify more or better than what or whom. The phrase "crushing the competition every day in every way" seems to mean something, but really doesn't. Calling a certain brand of liquor "the world's best-tasting vodka" doesn't make it a fact. Calling a car "the ultimate driving machine" doesn't make it so.

Any truth-in-advertising laws that still exist are shadows of what they should be. We are lied to every day by expert liars and truth spinners. Advertising and truth are often antithetical. Another typical outright lie is an ad that says "20 percent off," without specifying "off *what*"? If the answer can be specified truthfully—for example, "20 percent off what we've charged up until now" or "20 percent off what you'd pay at any of our competitors"—and that can be verified, fine. But all too often advertisers will arbitrarily pick a number and claim that their products are that percentage cheaper, without reference to any actual price, to make the consumer think he's getting a bargain. This is an example of what I call *pseudoinformation*. You're led to believe you're getting a discount, but there are no facts to back up the claim. A variation is the TV ad that states a product "normally sells for $50, but if you order now, you can get it for $19.99." Another example is the statement "we're selling below market cost," which implies that the seller isn't making a profit.

A specific example of pseudoinformation is Stanley Steemer's claim to get "your home cleaner." Cleaner than what? Sweeping the floor will also make your home cleaner. It's a statement that seems to mean something, but doesn't. Another meaningless statement is the tagline for the South Carolina Education Lottery: "Good luck, South Carolina!" Obviously, only a few of those who buy lottery tickets will be "lucky" winners. Hoping a specific individual wins has meaning, but to wish *everyone* luck is meaningless. Techniques like this blur the line between truth and deception. Ads for this lottery also tell people to "play smart," which I submit is an oxymoron. Lotteries have been rightfully called a tax on people who don't understand math. Gambling used to be regarded as an underground vice; now it is advertised and promoted as harmless fun.

Other deceptions include *lies of omission, card stacking,* and *distortion,* where facts are cherry-picked to promote the message and any contrary facts are left out or misrepresented; and a mixture of facts and lies, or half-truths, where facts are blended with opinions in a manner that tends to obscure the objective truth. When an ad claims that "nothing's been proven to beat" a product, that means only that the product is equal to its competitors, but the phrasing suggests it is superior.

Ad nauseam is the technique of repetition: "A lie repeated a thousand times becomes the truth." (This quote has been attributed to Joseph Goebbels, Hitler's propaganda minister.) *Transfer* is a term for creating an association, either positive or negative, between two unrelated things. Using the American flag as a backdrop for a political message is an example of positive transfer; a picture of a contemporary political figure with a Hitler mustache and a swastika in the background is an example of negative transfer. In psychology, this is a classical conditioning technique.

Another popular advertising technique is *bandwagon,* which suggests that we should follow the crowd, join the winning side, and avoid being left behind with the losers. *Glittering generalities* involves the use of emotionally loaded phrases, sometimes coupled with iconic images, that have no objective basis for definition: "national honor," "freedom lover," "true patriot," "perfect holiday," "best country in the world," etc. One man's freedom fighter is another man's terrorist.

Then there is *name calling*, which attempts to arouse prejudice or antipathy, sometimes in the form of unverified assertion—for example, Obama is a secret Muslim or socialist—sometimes in the form of sarcasm and ridicule. Name calling is related to *ad hominem*, in which someone attacks the messenger instead of responding to the message. *Plain folks*, which is related to bandwagon, is an attempt to convince the public that the views presented reflect the average person or "common sense." *Testimonial* and *appeal to authority* try to link endorsements, quotations (in or out of context), positions, or proposals with people viewed favorably by the target audience. For example, "Nine out of ten dentists recommend [a product]." Celebrity endorsements are in this category as are people who claim that their views would have been endorsed by Abraham Lincoln or Ronald Reagan. To suggest that one's agenda would have been endorsed by the Founding Fathers—or Jesus or Mohammed—is another example of appeal to authority.

Simplification and *pinpointing the enemy* offer simple explanations for complex issues and propose a culprit for an identified problem. Both approaches were used to devastating effect by the Nazis, to justify the mass murder of Jews. The *black-and-white fallacy* is also related: if you're not with us, you're against us; there is no middle ground. *Appeal to fear/prejudice* and *stereotyping* also belong to this cluster of propaganda techniques. "'Orientals' (Asians) are inscrutable and can't be trusted" is a classic example of a xenophobic stereotype.

Rhetorical Devices and Television Tactics

Rhetorical devices are also weapons in the propagandists' arsenal. Metaphor and simile have already been discussed. They are often accompanied and amplified by visual images. *Hyperbole* is exaggeration for effect and is a mainstay of commercial advertising. This can take the form of inflated claims of product efficacy or inflated woes. For example, there is a Lyrica ad in which someone suffering from diabetic nerve pain describes it as being like "a thousand bees stinging my feet," as though a hundred wouldn't communicate "it really hurts!" Sometimes the exaggeration is in visual form, as in Spiriva ads that suggest that chronic obstructive pulmonary disease feels like you have an elephant sitting on your chest. *Euphemism* softens and sweetens products for popular consumption; an example is "clean coal," an oxymoron if ever there was one.

Two other terms I've come up with to describe techniques frequently used in TV advertising are the *wow factor* and *straw dog*. The wow factor is a form of the transfer propaganda approach and the psychological principle of classical conditioning. When something in an ad—a beautiful woman, a boldly original animation, an amazing special effect—mesmerizes you or makes you go "wow!" you tend to form a positive association with the product or message. Repetition strengthens the association. Straw dog ads construct a fallacy and then easily knock it down. They define a problem—for example, your gray hair is keeping you from getting promoted or laid—and proceed to "solve" it with their product.

A recent commercial for Omega wristwatches combines the wow factor and transfer. It features an amazing animation of a clockwork world, taking you from a clockwork sea to a clockwork city with clockwork people. The music that accompanies the magical imagery is the soothing theme from *The Lord of the Rings* movies.

Infotoxins

My objections to advertising in contemporary society are two: volume and content. I see the constant encroachment of advertising in daily life as a pollution of the mental environment that has come to be regarded as normal. In his 1999 book *Culture Jam*, Kalle Lasn (1999, 18, 189) wrote about the effect of "infotoxins" on our culture:

> The commercial media are to the mental environment what factories are to the physical environment ... Advertisements are the most prevalent and toxic of the mental pollutants ... Culture isn't created from the bottom up by the people anymore—it's fed to us top-down by corporations.

We increasingly define ourselves by the products we consume.

As to content, I can tolerate informative ads, but my antennae go up when I catch the first whiff of propaganda. I resent attempts to deceive and manipulate me. During my studies in English (communication) and psychology, I examined the underlying structures and priorities in mass communication. Advertisers use focus groups and controlled studies and surveys to increase their effectiveness in manipulating mass behavior, and the industry wouldn't be as massive and pervasive as it is if its methods weren't effective, often at the subconscious level. They know that consumers often buy things on impulse and don't think about why until later, if at all. That's where heuristics fit into marketing strategy.

I get annoyed by advertising slogans and jingles that are designed to stick in our heads. And I resent the appropriation of some of my favorite pop and rock songs to promote products. Sometimes advertisers use popular tunes to create a positive association with their product, and sometimes they corrupt the lyrics, as when Minute Maid injected its corporate name into the lyrics of Stevie Wonder's "You Are the Sunshine of My Life" many years ago. I heard it over and over, and the song will never be the same to me.

Advertisers also appropriate iconic characters from other media to push products. The beloved *Peanuts* characters have been used to sell Dolly Madison cupcakes, A&W root beer, Kraft foods, Chex Mix, Cheerios, Bounty paper products, Met Life insurance, and Ford cars. In a recent car ad, Lucy appeared with adult actors, the first time I ever remember seeing a character from *Peanuts* with an adult. She jumped into the driver's seat of the car and pronounced it a cool ride. Superheroes have long been used to sell things, mostly to kids. I've been a Muppets fan for a long time, and it irks me to see them appropriated by advertisers to move merchandise. Now that the Muppet franchise is owned by Disney, I expect I'll see Muppets in advertisements for the rest of my life.

Art may influence at both the conscious and unconscious level, but true artists understand that their work will mean different things to different people. Propagandists may employ the methods and media of artists, but they have a specific message to sell and devious methods for accomplishing their goals. Freud's, Pavlov's, and Watson's teachings have led to the development of psychotechnologies of influence, and the advent of radio, cinema, television, and the Internet created new means of influencing behavior on a mass scale. The people who own and run the mass media are social engineers and have created a propaganda machine that has become, in the prescient words of Edward Bernays, father of PR, an "invisible government [that] is the true ruling power."

More Advertising Techniques

Ads often tell very short stories, with morals or solutions to the problems they pose. Such commercials usually feature an everyman (or everywoman) character (or two, as in ads for sexual nostrums), who either illustrates the benefits of using the product or service or offers advice. We are meant to identify with the everyman. He may be depicted overcoming a problem—dandruff, a leaky bladder, graying hair, psoriasis, etc.—by using the product being pitched, or he may address the viewers, describing how the product works or advising us that we need it.

Every December for the last few years, Aleve has shown a commercial that depicts Santa preparing for Christmas in his workshop; he is moving slowly and grimacing due to back pain. An elf looks at him sympathetically and doleful music runs in the background. Next we see Santa making a delivery, still in obvious pain. Everyman Dad leaves some Aleve for Santa, in lieu of cookies and milk. Then we see Santa back in his workshop, pain free and full of pep. The message is, if it works for Santa, it will work for you.

Here are some other advertising tactics I've identified;

there will be some overlap with the other concepts I've presented. *Big promises* tell you that a desired outcome is guaranteed, as in ChristianMingle's promise to find "God's match for you" and "The magic never has to stop at Disney World." An example of the *imperative voice* is "You need Restasis." *Advice/admonition* can take the form of prescriptions in the imperative voice ("Try ______"), clichés ("You deserve the best"), or reverse clichés ("You *can* have it all!"). *Flattering the customer* tells people "you deserve this," as in a magazine ad for Olympus cameras that states, "Introducing a camera as revolutionary as you are." Another example is "Get the credit you deserve!" *Cutesy* is similar to the wow factor described earlier, in that it tries to form a positive association with the product being advertised by making you think, "Aw, isn't that cute." It uses humor or whimsy and often involves kids or pets, although the ad may not be specifically targeted at children, parents, or pet owners.

A series of ads for AT&T shows a glib comedian sitting on the floor in a circle with young children, asking them loaded questions like, "Is fast better than slow?" and commenting whimsically on their cute responses. As a by-product, this series promotes such all-American values as "bigger or faster is better" and "two is better than one."

Learning Theory

Psychological learning theory posits two kinds of behavioral conditioning—classical conditioning and operant conditioning—and advertising uses both. Classical conditioning is associated with Pavlov's dogs, who were trained to salivate at the sound of a neutral stimulus (the ringing of a bell) because it was repeatedly paired with an unconditioned stimulus for salivation—for example, the presentation of food. A beautiful, sexy woman posing on the hood of a sports car at an automotive show is an example, as is a bikini-clad babe or a buff stud on a tropical beach in a beer commercial. Celebrity endorsements also create positive associations.

Classical conditioning is a passive mode of learning. Operant conditioning occurs when a behavior is reinforced (rewarded) in such a way to make people feel good about what they have done and to increase the likelihood that the behavior will be repeated. When people watching the Home Shopping Network succumb to a pitch and submit their orders, they feel satisfaction, imagining that they will soon possess the desired thing. Ads like the following example combine outright lies with the principles of operant conditioning: "If you call in the next twenty minutes, you'll get free shipping!" There's an expectation (or an illusion) of a reward, if you act right away.

Weapons of Influence

In his 1984 book *Influence: The New Psychology of Modern Persuasion*, social psychologist Robert Cialdini identifies six principles that could be applied as "weapons of influence" by "compliance practitioners." They can trigger automatic responses, mindless "fixed-action patterns" of behavior. The principles are consistency, reciprocation, social proof, authority, liking, and scarcity (Cialdini 1984, 13); and they can be correlated to some of the techniques of propaganda and the use of heuristics.

Consistency means that once we've made a commitment to a course of action, we tend to behave in a manner consistent with our initial commitment. This is exemplified by a salesperson who gets you to say yes to questions like, "Wouldn't you like to own a modern, state-of-the-art, labor-saving appliance that does all these things?" *Reciprocation* refers to the sense of obligation we feel when we perceive that another person has done something for us. It explains free samples of merchandise, and why many charities include a free token in their mailings. *Social proof* is a form of social modeling that suggests we take our cues from what others are doing. Nobody likes canned laughter in sitcoms, but it makes people laugh along and tends to improve a show's ratings

Authority has to do with our automatic response to symbols of authority, which is why ads use people wearing lab coats to promote medications. Ads using this principle often employ the imperative voice: "you should ... you must ..." *Liking* means that we're more inclined to be influenced by people we like and are attracted to, especially if we see them as similar to us. This explains why charming news reporters talk like they want to be your friend and "hope to see you again tomorrow night." *Scarcity* is the illusion of limited availability, as in "act now, while supplies last!" and "this week only!"

All these weapons of influence are employed by people whose business is persuasion. Recognizing them, as well as the techniques of propaganda, rhetoric, visual metaphors, heuristics, and behavior modification, will help you understand how advertising and public relations have become an effective engine of social engineering. Undergraduate and graduate programs in advertising teach students state-of-the-art methods of mass persuasion, covering all aspects of the trade. One university with a graduate program in marketing offers five majors: art direction, copywriting, communications strategy, creative brand management, and creative technology.

The propagandist's tools are used tactically to move merchandise, sell services, and win votes. But advertising campaigns are planned strategically, often based on market research. While it's beyond the scope of this book to comprehensively examine marketing strategies, I'll briefly reflect on some aspects of branding.

Branding

Branding is an important component of strategic marketing. It has to do with establishing a corporate identity and promoting brand loyalty. The American Marketing Association defines branding as "a name, term, design, symbol or any other feature that identifies one seller's good or service as distinct from those of other sellers."

In his 2010 book, *Brand Society,* Martin Kornberger (2010, 175) writes, "Brands ... provide the raw material that we use to build our individual lifestyles." In other words, to marketers you are what you buy. According to Kornberger, "The rise of marketing as a discipline started in the 1930s as competition and consumer spending increased. This development marks the birth of the consumer society that forms the bedrock of our lives" (Kornberger 2010, 178). As Sidney Levy, professor emeritus of marketing and behavioral science in management at the Kellogg School of Management put it, "A consumer's personality can be seen as the peculiar total of the products he consumes" (Kornberger 2010, 191).

One of the frequent aims of branding is to persuade consumers that a particular product or service is the only one that will satisfy their needs or provide a solution to their particular problems. Another branding tactic is to get consumers to connect the product with their own personal styles or identities. While blind trials or taste tests often reveal that few consumers can distinguish their favorite brand from its competitors, merchandisers only need to create a perception that their brand is superior to others, or the best one for you, to establish brand loyalty and keep you coming back for more. Advertising giant David Ogilvy suggested that an inexpensive bourbon will taste better to most people if they're told that it is top of the line. He called it "tasting images."

I can't tell you why, but when I was a cigarette smoker I smoked Benson & Hedges, year after year. They didn't taste noticeably different from other brands, but they seemed to fit my self-image or identity, in a way that Marlboros or Virginia Slims didn't. Perhaps it was the monochrome gold pack and the cosmopolitan cachet of the British-sounding name. It may even have been due to a four-year advertising blitz that increased sales sevenfold.

I imagine that most Marlboro smokers are men, and that they consciously or unconsciously identify with the Marlboro Man. Virginia Slims are clearly marketed to women who want to be slender, and I suspect that when they went on the market they were popular among women who identified themselves as liberated women and feminists.

Association

One branding strategy is to associate the product with a sport or some other activity with fans. Some ads have invited consumers to affiliate themselves with a sponsor-created affinity group, to actually make a commitment to brand loyalty. Such an ad, for Winston cigarettes, appeared in the 2000 *Sports*

Illustrated swimsuit issue, aimed at NASCAR fans. "We are the citizens of the Winston Racing Nation," it proclaimed. "Join us." Stephen Colbert has cleverly parodied this branding tactic with his Colbert Nation.

Successful branding tactics imbue the product with credibility and seek to connect with consumers on an emotional level, motivating them to be loyal to the product. Perhaps addressing the growing antismoking movement and the consequent restrictions on smoking and tobacco advertising, the Winston ad sought to characterize the "citizens of the Winston Racing Nation," using the emotionally laden statement, "We are free" (presumably to smoke their way to an early grave). Other slogans that attempt to connect with consumers on the emotional level are McDonald's "We do it all for you" and Subaru's "Love—it's what makes a Subaru a Subaru."

Another ploy is to get the consumer to associate the product with celebrity or achievement. Famous actors endorse products and services, and the Wheaties box has long been a showcase for popular athletes.

Logos, Symbols, and Slogans

Two of the most important elements in establishing a brand identity are the logo and the slogan. A distinctive logo is an instant ad for the brand, whether it appears on a sign or on someone's T-shirt. The appearance of the logo on the product itself might heighten the prestige of owning it, increase its snob appeal. Some of the cleverest brandings combine the logo and slogan in an unforgettable way, as with the Energizer Bunny who keeps on going and going and going. Other slogans suggest that using a product will provide a transcendent emotional experience, like Coke's "Open happiness" and Disney's "happiest place on earth."

Some slogans are pitched at a niche market, like Harley-Davidson's "American by birth. Rebel by choice" and Calvin Klein's "Between love and madness lies Obsession." An effective slogan is one that sticks in your head and is distinctively associated with a particular brand. We all know who does it all for us, who lets you have it your way, what not to leave home without, what's good to the very last drop, who wants you to just do it, what the breakfast of champions is, what to send when you care to send the very best, what pours when it rains, and what Ajax is stronger than.

There are other methods for establishing a brand personality—from distinctive packaging (e.g., Campbell's Soup's red-and-white cans) to clever use of imagery (Absolut Vodka's visual puns in its magazine ads) to the creation of iconic characters. For years the bored Maytag repairman pitched us on the product line's reliability. Flo, the chipper girl-next-door-in-white, cajoles us on behalf of Progressive Insurance, in an imaginary white-on-white insurance emporium.

Sane Advertising Revisited

A single, simple major step in the direction of sane advertising would be a strict truth-in-advertising law with teeth. Such a law would specify that opinions couldn't be presented as facts in advertising. Period. Violators of the law would be forced to stop their deceptive practices or be penalized. In my opinion, the Federal Trade Commission (FTC) and the Federal Communications Commission (FCC) are watchdogs that no longer have teeth.

It used to be that the ratio of advertising to program

content was regulated. Now we have hour-long infomercials and programming that's interrupted every few minutes with several minutes of ads. A society with sane advertising would establish something like a 1:12 ratio—five minutes of ads per hour of broadcasting. All the ads would be in blocks at the beginning and the end of shows, or during intermissions, if there were natural breaks in the program and the ads didn't violate the program's integrity. A five-act Shakespeare play would allow for four natural commercial breaks as well as commercials before and after. Ideally, the pricing of ads wouldn't be determined by ratings. This would encourage quality programming, as opposed to a competition to find the lowest common denominator, in a race to the bottom.

Given that advertising at its best can provide helpful information, and stimulate innovation and healthy competition in the marketplace, I don't advocate its abolition. I just think that the world would be a better place if it were better regulated, and I wish that propaganda techniques were routinely taught in public schools. Democracies thrive on truth and fact-based debate and weaken on a steady diet of propaganda.

Whom Does Propaganda Serve?

Whom does propaganda serve? The easy answer is usually "the people who pay for it," although in the case of some public service campaigns, the public can be served. Successful mass advertisements that rely on the techniques of propaganda yield results, whether in sales figures or votes. Anyone with paper or poster board and a pencil or a crayon can produce propaganda, but it generally requires substantial money to produce powerful campaigns that take your persuasive message to the masses effectively.

Propaganda in advertising serves materialism, consumerism, and, in our society, capitalism. It creates needs we didn't know we had and stimulates our appetite for new possessions. It creates a noisy mental environment where facts, lies and half-truths, glitzy images, and persuasion techniques are skillfully blended to shape mass behavior. In such an environment, one can find such brands as Philosophy Cosmetics smoothly homogenizing the profound and the superficial. The Massage Envy chain employs one of the seven deadly sins to market its product. Hipness is marketed as a commodity, and Zen is for sale.

Bread and circuses, Juvenal's recipe for keeping the masses content, has morphed into pizza and cable. If cable and dish TV service and home delivery of pizza were curtailed for a protracted period, social unrest would surely ensue. Edward Bernays's "invisible government" has made a science of the prediction and control of mass behavior. Docile consumers are more easily managed than well-informed citizens. George Orwell couldn't have imagined that Big Brother might wear an Armani suit.

Orwell's essay "Politics and the English Language" (1956, 355) discusses the purposeful manipulation of words—a topic also addressed in his novels *Animal Farm* and *1984*—stating that "the decline of language must ultimately have political and economic causes ... The slovenliness of our language makes it easier to have foolish thoughts." As examples of politicized language he cites such euphemisms as "pacification" and "rectification of frontiers" (Orwell 1956, 363).

Orwell (1956, 364) goes on to say, "This invasion of one's mind by ready-made phrases ... can only be prevented if one is constantly on guard against them, and every such phrase anaesthetizes a portion of one's brain." He concludes that "political language ... is designed to make lies sound truthful and murder respectable, and to give the appearance of solidity to pure wind" (Orwell 1956, 366).

The Unconscious Mind

Now I'll briefly cover the topics of the unconscious mind, hypnotism, brainwashing, and systems theory as they relate to advertising. Sigmund Freud believed that much of human behavior is governed by unconscious desires and motivations, and that sometimes the id—the selfish, willful child within each of us—rules. Id impulses that demand gratification can influence sexual behavior and other forms of pleasure seeking but also often affect such mundane things as shopping behavior. Studies have suggested that if you go food shopping on an empty stomach, you're likely to buy more food than if you'd shopped with your belly full.

Edward Bernays realized that the principles his uncle introduced could be exploited by commercial propagandists, both in advertising and in public relations. Classic propaganda techniques aim below the level of conscious, logical thought, and appeal to us at a gut level, whether they're used to influence our buying choices or our votes.

Unconscious manipulation techniques can target our wishes or our fears. Some advertisements suggest that a product will enable us to fulfill our desires, and others reassure us that our flaws can be overcome. The most effective TV ads are those that combine arresting visual imagery with carefully chosen words; sometimes the visuals predominate, and at other times, it's the words. The skillful combination of words and images for the purpose of influencing mass behavior has become a social science, as Bernays predicted.

Hypnotism

There's no absolute definition of hypnotism, and there are several theories or models to explain the hypnotic state of consciousness. The most prevalent model posits that an induction produces a trance state, in which the subject is susceptible to suggestion. The trance can be induced by words or images and other sensory cues. So is hypnotism a relevant term in a book about the psychology of advertising?

Not really. One could argue that infomercials can have a hypnotic effect, as they are designed to command the viewers' sustained attention to a persuasive message. A good pitchman, it could be argued, can induce a trancelike state designed to make the consumer susceptible to suggestion. But most ads, interspersed with unrelated programming, are too short to induce a trance state, and there are too many messages competing for the consumer's attention in the media marketplace. However, it can be argued that watching TV may induce a generalized trance state.

Brainwashing

Although some might characterize the bombardment of mass media advertising as brainwashing, I won't use that term in my criticisms of advertising and public relations. Although brainwashing utilizes some of the techniques of propaganda (notably card stacking, distortion, and ad nauseam), true brainwashing requires that the subject be isolated from all contrary messages. Brainwashing can't tolerate competing messages, and mass media advertising is all about competing messages.

Systems Theory

Systems theory is a way of understanding how whole systems operate. One application of systems theory is cybernetics, the science of self-regulating systems. An example of a self-regulating system is a thermostat-controlled heating and air-conditioning system in an indoor environment. The thermostat is set to maintain a temperature within the 70–73 degree range, which we'll call a steady state (a desired state of equilibrium within the system). The agent of change in systems theory is information or feedback.

In the summer, the heat from outside, which raises the temperature inside, would be labeled deviation-enhancing feedback because it takes us away from the defined steady state. When the inside heat rises above 73 degrees, the air conditioner turns on and pumps in cool air—that is, deviation-reducing feedback—until the temperature falls below 70 degrees, and it turns off. In the winter, the cold outside air would be the deviation-enhancing feedback, and heat from the furnace would be deviation-reducing feedback.

The systems theory model can be applied to biological organisms, communication, and social units ranging from family to community to society. In biology, steady state can be expressed as homeostasis, a state of balance and wellness in the organism or system. If a person's system is invaded by a microorganism that upsets the homeostatic balance (deviation-enhancing feedback), he might develop a fever (deviation-reducing feedback) that lasts only long enough to kill off the invader and restore homeostasis.

Applied to communication, in a discussion between two people who disagree about a topic, the steady state might be defined as civil discourse. A vicious ad hominem attack—"You're an unprincipled idiot!"—in a formal debate would be seen as deviation-enhancing feedback. If the other person responded with a loud counterattack rant, that would be further deviation-enhancing feedback. If, instead, he or she responded in a moderate tone, commenting pointedly on the opponent's attack without attacking back, that would be deviation-reducing feedback.

Systems theory has applications in family therapy, when the family is viewed as a system. Parents may take a child in for counseling as the identified patient, because the child's behavior presents an insoluble problem within the family. A family systems therapist would view the child's problem as a symptom of family dysfunction and address it at the level of the family system and effective parental responses, without saddling the child with the label of "the cause of the family's problem." A good example is a child who throws tantrums. Typically, tantrums only persist when the parents or caretakers unwittingly reinforce the behavior by their responses to it. Change the family system's response in such a way that the behavior is no longer being reinforced, and the tantrums usually stop.

Communities and nations also can be studied and understood through the lens of systems theory. A change in one aspect of a system can lead to an automatic adjustment to that change throughout the system. Think about how the single issue of voters' rights has affected our democracy in the last century. If the steady state was maintenance of the status quo of white male dominance, then the female suffrage and the civil rights movements can be seen as deviation-enhancing feedback. Now that women and minorities generally have fair access to the polls—a free flow of information or feedback—the system has changed fundamentally. There is a new normal.

How is systems theory relevant to my thesis? Signal versus noise ratio is a factor in systems theory, in regard to deviation-enhancing or reducing information or feedback. Signal is defined as information you can use; noise is useless information—loud static. One person's noise is another person's signal. How much of what you perceive via the mass media on an average day is information you can use? How much is clutter?

I am inundated by commercial noise on a daily basis. Most of the ads I see and hear promote products I'm not in the market for; they're noise. Every sign I see advertising a business establishment that's out of business, every "open" sign on the door of a closed joint, every political poster still on display after an election is noise. Every hyperbolic claim that is pitched to me by a media salesperson is noise. This constant barrage of noise is a form of mental pollution; it takes a toll on our attention to detail and fact and blurs the lines between truth and fiction, the natural and the manufactured.

If republican democracy is viewed as a system, its maintenance of a steady state—defined as rule by the people—depends on an educated and well-informed electorate. A democratic system thrives on the free flow of accurate information. Mass deception and manipulation undermine the principles by which true democracy is preserved. The advertising industry often makes citizens more distracted and malleable, content as long as they get their pizza and cable. It warps what we call the news. Kalle Lasn (1999, 34) wrote, "The looming presence of big advertisers influences, if only subconsciously, every executive decision made in every newsroom across North America."

If it's true that many Americans care more about who wins the Super Bowl or triumphs on *American Idol* or *Survivor* than they care about who's behind the curtain in the political arena, that's no accident. The capitalists who control the mass media seem to have an agenda that is antithetical to the ideal notion of a free press, one of the pillars of democracy. To the degree that advertisers directly or indirectly exert influence on journalistic content, the press isn't truly free. Given the growing popularity of product placement, not even entertainment programming is commercial free.

Situationalism

According to situationalism, a postmodern movement popularized in the 1960s by Guy Debord in France, we live in a world of manufactured situations and spectacles, and our experiences are marketed as commodities. Spectacles—arena events, theme parks, resorts, cruises, 3-D Imax movies, multimedia extravaganzas, or spectacular TV programming—distract us from the real, the natural, the authentic. All these together constitute one great Spectacle.

I thought I'd coined the term Disneyfication in the 1970s, but then I heard other people using it. Apparently, it was a term whose time had come. Simulated stimulation or adventure is available to anyone with the money to pay for a momentary distraction from the mundane, difficult, and ugly. When we're fixated on the Spectacle, we're being programmed not to notice who's behind the curtain, running the show. Advertising is critical to the maintenance of the Spectacle, offering us a wide selection of diversions, from the latest blockbuster movie to vacation packages on a Caribbean island theme resort called Atlantis or at American meccas of fun, like Orlando and Las Vegas. We're pitched by beloved cartoon characters and promised packaged thrills with our favorite superheroes. For the price of admission, we can feel like we've entered the *Star Wars* universe or Jurassic Park. We can experience the illusion of taking risks and cheating death, without leaving our seats or breaking a sweat. Disneyworld, we're told, is a "magic kingdom."

Political Propaganda

The people who own and run the mass media seem to have an agenda that is not conducive to the maintenance of democracy. Our opinions and our behaviors are commodities to them. They use polls, focus groups, and controlled studies to refine their technologies of influence. They've conditioned consumers to the point where it's normal to be inundated by propaganda and not even notice its effects on us. Most of the propaganda we're exposed to on a daily basis is commercial advertising, but political propaganda has proliferated over the years. Political propagandists work on the assumption that, in this thoroughly propagandized society, perception frequently trumps truth.

Tear Down This Wall

A classic example of a political public relations coup was the selling of the notion that Ronald Reagan brought the Soviet Union to its knees when he told the Soviets to "tear down this [Berlin] wall." This trick was akin to the plot device in H.

Rider Haggard's 1885 novel *King Solomon's Mines* in which Allan Quatermain, surrounded by savages, uses his knowledge of astronomy to save his skin. Knowing that there's about to be a solar eclipse, he threatens to make the sun go dark. When it does, the savages are awed into submission, believing that our hero caused the phenomenon.

It had been clear to me for years that the Soviet Union was doomed, a rotten fruit that would fall from the tree sooner or later. Conversations with a close friend who worked at the Pentagon as an army intelligence officer specializing in the Soviet Union confirmed my belief that it was only a matter of time. President Reagan's "demand" that the Berlin Wall come down was perfectly timed to make it seem that he was responsible for the predictable, inevitable collapse of the Soviet system. The whole trick was in the timing. The Soviet Union would have fallen apart around that time no matter who was in the White House, or what he said.

Swiftboating

I can't think of a better example of political campaign propaganda than the swiftboat ad campaign mounted against presidential candidate John Kerry in 2004, underwritten by a Texas multimillionaire right-winger. There is no doubt that Kerry served honorably in combat in Viet Nam, but many hawks never forgave him for his subsequent criticisms of the war, capitalizing on his status as an honorably discharged and decorated combat veteran. The swiftboat ads used classic audiovisual propaganda techniques, combining a rapid sequence of images and words to dramatic effect, to suggest that Kerry hadn't served honorably and was an unpatriotic liar. The truth proved to be less important to the public than the perception that his service was somehow tainted.

Meanwhile, the controversy over George W. Bush's military service led to the downfall of distinguished TV journalist Dan Rather, purely due to the manipulation of perception. There are questions that remain unanswered about whether Bush faithfully fulfilled the terms of his military contract. There's good reason to believe he may have gotten away with absences from duty, due to the family ties that got him into the Texas Air National Guard, sparing him from being sent to Viet Nam. He may have skipped out on some of his military obligations and was exempt from normal accountability, because everyone knew who his daddy was.

I think there must be some truth to these allegations of a dereliction of duty by a son of privilege, as Bush's team wasn't able to find a single person who was able to say "I have documentation that I was there at the time in question, and can personally verify that Lieutenant Bush was there too." But Rather's reputation and job went down the tubes overnight because some documents that he had confidence in, pertaining to Bush's military service, had been forged. It's not that Dan Rather was proven to be a fraud, but suddenly he was perceived as untrustworthy. Right-wing propagandists drove him into journalistic exile.

The irony for me is that Kerry, who unquestionably met his military obligation, was pilloried by right-wing propagandists in the mass media, while Bush has been given every benefit of the doubt by the press. If the campaign against Kerry was successful in achieving its immediate goal of discrediting him in the public eye, it failed in the sense that it called attention to the propaganda techniques it utilized, immortalized as "swiftboating." It failed the ideal propaganda standard of invisibility and survives as a textbook example of an ad campaign that's unfair and untrue, but nevertheless effective.

Political campaigns have long used propaganda, but the stakes have been raised. Due to the arms race effect, negative political ads have become the norm, substituting simplistic slogans and propagandistic criticism of the opponent for discussion of relevant issues or promotion, in any detail, of the candidate's agenda. This trend undermines political dialogue and ultimately the democratic process.

How Advertising Changed Everything

In a simpler time, the influence of advertising was limited by the available technologies: signs, pamphlets, ads in periodicals, etc. With the advent of mass media such as radio, cinema, TV, the Internet, smartphones, and tablets, the advertising industry has become one of the most potent forces that shapes society. The term *social engineers* has been used for years by conservatives who state that it is not the role of government to promote social agendas, but I submit that the whole purpose of the advertising and public relations industries is to shape behavior on a mass scale—social engineering. If it didn't work, there wouldn't be so much of it. The Public Relations Society of America presents Silver Anvil awards for success in "forging public opinion." That sounds like social engineering to me.

In the following pages I intend to focus first on print advertising, telephones, movies, signs and billboards, television, radio, and the Internet. Then I'll cover sports, nutrition and medicine, health, education and child rearing, law and politics, religion and spirituality, popular culture, and the environment, as they're interconnected in our media-dominated society. If it's true that advertising and public relations have fundamentally changed practically every aspect of American life, it didn't just happen. Our collective acceptance of a world made up of commodities and spectacles has been carefully engineered by experts in the field of mass persuasion, Bernays's "invisible government."

Unless you live off the grid, advertising is inescapable, and advertisers are always finding new ways to bring their messages to our attention. We are fed commercial messages in the form of print ads; telephone solicitations and robocalls; commercials on TV, radio, and the Internet; and signs, posters, and billboards. There are video monitors that pitch the lottery at checkout counters; ads on the handles of shopping carts; cars and other vehicles that are mobile billboards; little speakers pitching you while you pump at some gas stations; and more ads popping up in new places all the time. I've even seen advertising on rubber pads in urinals. We're a captive audience wherever we go, whatever we do.

In stage magic, the term *Hobson's choice* means forcing a card on someone who thinks he chose that card. When public relations pros contend that they're only giving consumers what they want, they are playing Hobson's card, dealt from Hobson's deck at Hobson's casino.

Although we've been told for years that the liberal elite control the media, in fact it is owned and controlled by corporate America. While something like fifty corporations controlled most US media outlets in the early 1980s, today it's down to a handful (Media Reform Information Center).

Ninety-six percent of the information and entertainment content we have available to us (periodicals, books, radio, TV, and movies) now comes from six corporations: Time Warner, Viacom, CBS, Walt Disney, News Corp, and GE (Floyd 2013).

The political right wing has accused those who favor taxing the rich at a high rate as waging "class warfare." But if you look at the progressive wage gap between the rich and the rest of us over the past half-century, it's clear who's been successfully waging a class war against whom. The PR and advertising industries have played a major role as social engineers in this redistribution of wealth to the wealthy, especially in the arena of political advertising.

Every major military establishment in the modern world puts money into research and development, hoping to be able to invent and exploit the latest weapons technologies to its tactical and strategic benefit. One area of interest to military research and development is known as psychological operations (psyops): the use of media, propaganda techniques and disinformation technologies as psychological weapons in warfare. In psyops, perceptions trump facts, and the end justifies the means. Truth, according to Aeschylus, is the first casualty of war, and propaganda is a major weapon in the psyops arsenal.

It would be naive to believe that these same techniques and psychotechnologies are not a part of the class war that much of the upper class has waged against the rest of us. The very rich own and control the mass media, employ the best propagandists money can buy, and systematically use Nielsen ratings and focus groups and market research to help them refine their techniques of mass behavior manipulation. It is in their perceived interest to blur the lines between fact and opinion, to promulgate disinformation, and to distract us with the Spectacle.

We consumers are commodities. (See appendix 1, “On Commodities.”) Advertisers study us, use the data to categorize us in ways that are useful to merchandisers, and then trade and sell that data, targeting us for sales pitches on a variety of media, geared to our demographic and consumer profiles. Data mining is a profitable enterprise, and sophisticated programs track our web browsing and online shopping patterns to determine what ads to send to us in the future.

Part 1: The Media

Print Advertising

Print advertising—that is, the fliers that get delivered with the newspaper or as junk mail—is a wasteful, inefficient enterprise, contributing both to deforestation and pollution from paper mills. I wonder how many pounds of inked paper are produced per person in the United States each year, much of it tossed, unread. We get print ads in periodicals, and as print newspapers continue to struggle for survival in the media market, the ratio of advertising to content has increased in many of them. In some papers you have to thumb through pages thick with ads to make sure you do not miss an article. Some ads are disguised to look like news articles, and stickers adorn the masthead on the front page. And in addition there are the fliers, often duplicates of them. The thickness of my Sunday paper is now due more to fliers, brochures and mini-catalogs than to newspaper. Almost all such printed matter is useless in my household, trashed unread. What a waste.

Advertising wizards know the break-even point, where it's worthwhile to print one hundred thousand color inserts for the Sunday paper, even if they know that (theoretically) only 37 percent will be perused by a consumer, only 63 percent of whom will purchase an advertised item. Most of the print run is wasted paper and ink, and it all ends up in a recycling bin or landfill. But not all the advertising that comes with the paper is in the form of supplements.

Advertorials

Advertorials appear on TV as well as in periodicals, often in the form of infomercials. In print, advertorials are ads designed to simulate journalism and editorial content—stealth advertising, designed to fly beneath the radar of consumer scrutiny. They mimic objective reportage; they are ads in camouflage.

Print advertorials often tout breakthroughs in medicine or health care. Interspersed with the news articles they resemble, they carry the cachet of truthful reportage, even though they use terms like *anti-aging* that have no basis in fact. A recent two-page ad for a product called SeroVital-hgh, which claims to stimulate the body's production of human growth hormones (HGH), appeared in *Parade* and the *New York Times Magazine* (March 24, 2013). Over the second page there's a small supertitle—"Advertisement"—but otherwise the ad appears to be an article. The highlighted text at the top of the first page is "Anti-Aging News" in red and "Special Report" in blue. The headline reads, "Turn Back Time with the 'Anti-aging' Breakthrough Everyone Is Talking About!" The byline explains that the writer is Tiffany Strobel, who is credited as "an author, columnist and beauty editor." The ad suggests that some of the "rich and famous of Beverly Hills" call HGH the "Fountain of Youth," and that unspecified "experts ... believe it's the key to combating aging." It states that SeroVital-hgh "encourages the pituitary gland to increase growth hormone production," which "experts" believe "reduces body fat, increases lean muscle mass, boosts mood, heightens sex drive ... and gets rid of wrinkles." The author writes, "the 'established' medical community (and, of course, they know everything) would say that its benefits are largely anecdotal ..." but concludes that "something that has a chance of making you look and feel ... *decades* younger is ... irresistible." This is faux journalism.

A half-page ad in the form of an article appeared on page 3 of a recent edition of the Columbia, SC, *State* newspaper. It began with the heading, "Health & Medicine" and stated, "This tiny pill could put your doctor out of business by 2014! Florida company develops what experts call 'the end of medicine.'" The ad suggests that the product, BactiPlus, can cure joint discomfort, stomach disorders, and other chronic conditions. It states that the research on the product is the "biggest medical news in decades," and that BactiPlus "could be the most important discovery since penicillin." The byline identifies the author as Stephanie Wechsler, credited as a "freelance health editor." She introduces us to "America's most trusted pharmacist," Dr. Earl Mindell, who envisions "a world where almost nobody gets sick." The ad states that health problems start in the colon and that keeping a clean colon could "add more than a decade to your life." Mindell, we're told, is convinced that if all Americans took BactiPlus, "90% of hospitals would shut down." Unspecified "experts," we are told, agree with the ad's claims. Yet a box beneath the ad includes the statement that the claims haven't been evaluated by the Food and Drug Administration (FDA), and "these products are not intended to diagnose, treat, cure or prevent any disease." You could have fooled me.

Tiffany Strobel and Stephanie Wechsler are presented as journalists, rather than as writers of ad copy. Their job is not to inform you, but to persuade you, by making their respective ads appear to be news articles—advertorials. Not all advertising is innately deceptive, but this kind is. Such deceptive advertising would be illegal if we had truth-in-advertising laws that actually required advertisers to be truthful in their claims. Apparently ads for medical nostrums can make whatever claims they want, as long as they print the standard disclaimer, which is usually in tiny print at the bottom of the ad.

Big Promises

A recent full-page color ad in *Free Times* advertised a "male enhancement" product named Vixalis: all-natural nonprescription pills that are guaranteed not only to produce immediate, "durable" erections and heightened sexual desire, but to also rapidly and dramatically increase penis size, giving the user a "newfound sexual mastery." Such ads target men with anxiety, whether justified or not, about their sexual performance. The Vixalis ad promises a simple solution to perceived inadequacy as well as a new sexual confidence. ("No more doubting yourself!") And because it doesn't claim to treat a medical disorder, no FDA disclaimer is required. Opinions presented as facts are a form of constitutionally protected free speech, no proof required.

The *New Yorker* recently featured a full-page ad for Gravity Defyer shoes, "scientifically engineered to defy gravity." The ad states that wearing these shoes will make you "feel weightless" and that they're guaranteed to "change your life." A full-page ad in the *State* newspaper ran the headline, "Thousands stand to miss deadline to claim free US silver coins." The advertorial touts vault bags of "free" silver coins "up for grabs." All you have to do to claim your free coins is pay a $149 "vault bag fee." Any resemblance between advertising and truth is optional.

Junk Mail

Another form of print advertising is called direct mail by the industry, but is known popularly as junk mail. It accounts for much of the mail delivered by the Postal Service these days. My family certainly gets its share, but hardly any of the letters, pamphlets, fliers, notices, and special offers we get ever result in a sale. We're still on the Publishers Clearing House mailing list, and we still get promises that we can "save thousands" on a new car if we act now. We buy an occasional college course from the Teaching Company, then get catalog after catalog before we finish it and are potentially in the market for another one. We regularly get a catalog for homeowners with swimming pools, although we don't have a pool. Waste. Noise.

Purveyors of junk mail use tricks to get you to open the envelope. They use official-looking envelopes, often with names that suggest a government-affiliated agency. They typically bear messages like "urgent" or "action required." "Do not bend" suggests that there is something of value inside that you wouldn't want to destroy, and increases the odds that you'll open the envelope. (It's usually a bookmark.) Publishers Clearing House (PCH) mailings include a statement that you won't increase your odds of winning by subscribing to a magazine, but they know that many recipients don't read the fine print and still order magazine subscriptions because they think it *will* increase their odds. The ad copy suggests that somehow your odds are better than average and otherwise implies a high likelihood of your winning. One such example plays on the reader's family responsibilities: "Don't let yourself and your loved ones down! Respond today to go for a real legacy-making win—$5,000 every week 'forever.'" Since "forever" is in quotes, you know that it will not *really* be forever.

I got a PCH mailing some time ago and tossed it. Then I got a follow-up solicitation in an oversized envelope, covered with ersatz labels, hand stamps and handwritten messages, to get my attention. I'm used to messages persuasively soliciting my entry in the sweepstakes, but this mailing was a hard sell. The copy frequently employed the imperative voice, ordering me to do things, and had an almost bullying tone in places. The only real sticker on the envelope was in red and white block letters: "Notice Re 'Winning Number Found' Report." A fake hand stamp read, "Action Required." A fake sticker (actually a printed part of the envelope) appeared to slightly overlap a printed box with two red arrows pointing to the headline, "Time-sensitive Deadline Critical" and the following text: "Failure to complete a valid entry for your Personal Prize Number enclosed may be cause for serious concern. If you miss the entry deadline and this number is a match to the winning number, it will automatically appear on the 'Winning Number Not Found' report, and you will have no further claim to any prize money it could have won." The fake sticker had the headline "Imminent Forfeiture Warning" and beneath it the name Jeffrey Koob. Below that, the text read: "You've ignored prior Bulletins and are hereby forewarned not to do it again. You must open and respond by the deadline to give your Prize Number its chance to be found. Five Thousand Dollars Every Week Forever is at stake. Forfeiture for nonresponse is permanent and cannot be reversed. We'll be awaiting your response. Don't delay!"

Or what? The Prize Patrol will show up at my house with rope and rubber truncheons?

The most devious ploy is the threat of "imminent forfeiture" if I don't respond by the deadline, when in fact I will forfeit nothing (except perhaps fantasies of winning). Everything in this mailing is an elaboration of the obvious fact: if you don't enter, you can't win. But look at all the methods they use to hammer this home and to get you to respond. They tell you that it's critical for you to respond, implying that you may let down your family if you don't. They make the mailing seem personal, as if it were sent by someone who really cares about you and your family and wants you to win. (This hypothetical human will be looking to see if *your* winning number is *the* winning number.) They chastise you for ignoring them in the past and "forewarn" you not to do it again. They notify you that you're facing a "critical deadline," and failure to respond will be a "cause for serious concern." They personify your unique prize number and tell you that you must respond in order to give it a "chance to be found." They tell you that your imminent forfeiture is permanent and irreversible, which is just another way of saying that you can't win this particular sweepstakes if you don't enter. But they make it sound like you'll be forever forfeiting the fantasy of windfall wealth that helps them sell magazines; you'll be banished from the PCH fantasyland "forever."

And that's just the envelope. Inside are further imperative messages: admonishments not to forfeit my prize number and to "return this form," and a reminder that my action is required. There are also what appear to be scratch-and-win game cards, but are actually there to encourage you to enter the sweepstakes or to order merchandise displayed on the many pages of ads that accompanied the sweepstakes material.

Other Print Ads

If you once buy something from a mail-order merchant, you'll probably stay on its catalogue mailing list for a while. Catalogues can be fun to browse, if they're your kind of catalogue, but in our home they tend to stack up in piles if they're not thrown out right away. Although catalogues tend to be straightforward consumer guides—if sometimes riddled with hyperbole—the noise-to-signal ratio is enormous. I'd estimate that we get several pounds of catalogues for any single purchase we might make. They represent another extremely wasteful means of selling.

I am a regular reader of our local (Columbia, SC) free weekly *Free Times*. Free independent periodicals depend on heavy advertising, but I'm willing to put up with it because I like the journalistic content and the features. And occasionally I might learn about a local restaurant or business establishment. Thus, I'm not completely opposed to print ads. They have their place, but I think there are just too many of them. Sad to say, without them daily print newspapers probably would have passed into history years ago.

The Telephone

Largely unregulated by the federal government, the telephone advertising industry's tactics became so intolerable that the people demanded relief from dinnertime solicitations, robocalls, and other invasive telephone-marketing schemes. A do-not-call list was established. While this has cut down the volume of telephone solicitations, there are still advertisers who manage to get around the rules. Many robocalls are deceptive "phishing" calls, designed to get credit card information for the purpose of identity theft. We get one on a recurring basis that tells us there's an unspecified problem with "your credit card account," without specifying a card, and asks us to call and straighten it out. If there's a law against this deceptive practice, it isn't being enforced.

Politicians and charities are exempt from the restrictions of the no-call list. I expect that we get fewer charity solicitations on the phone than many households, because for years we've hung up on all robocalls and have had a standard response to any and all telephone solicitations: "We don't accept any kind of telephone solicitations. Please take us off your list." That's usually enough to get a polite response acknowledging our declaration. But if the caller is rude enough to persist, we hang up. Unwanted calls remain an aggravation, despite regulation.

Advertisers are always looking for new captive audiences. It's bad enough to be put on hold when I'm navigating an automated phone system, waiting to speak to a real, live person; but my aggravation is compounded when I'm subjected to commercial messages that I can only escape from by hanging up.

At this writing I still don't have my own cell phone, nor do I want one. I'm glad my wife has one, in case of emergencies; but we don't have children, and I like not always being reachable by phone. Thus, I can't cite specifics about the incursions of advertising into web searches and other online services available on smartphones from personal experience, but I know what it's like when I'm online on my computer. The bottom line is that you can't access certain things without first viewing advertisements. There's no ad-free alternative.

I'll admit that it's a trade-off, like tolerating all the ads that make *Free Times* free. If I have to endure a ten-second ad in order to watch a music video on YouTube for free, I can't say it's all bad. But it's just one more stream in the torrent of advertising that pummels me daily. I wish I had the option to pay a few dollars a month for access to the YouTube library and other web resources, and skip the ads. And I suspect that we'll see an upward creep of the ad-to-content ratio over time, as has happened on TV. One thing is for sure. Advertisers will get away with as much mental manipulation as they can, if they're not regulated.

A manipulative form of political advertising via telephone is the push poll. When you answer the phone, the caller identifies himself or herself as a pollster who wants to ask you some questions. In fact, it's not really a poll, and the questions are designed to surreptitiously shape or sway your opinion regarding some issue or political candidate. These faux polls employ some of the propaganda techniques used in negative political ads on TV, to leave you with the desired impression or to make you think you know something in order to influence your opinion.

Movies

Movies have been used for propaganda purposes since early in the twentieth century. D. W. Griffith's silent film *Birth of a Nation* was a cinematic masterpiece of its time, but it might as well have been a recruiting film for the Ku Klux Klan. *Reefer Madness* was a propaganda film that portrayed marijuana as the devil's weed, and served to reinforce the prohibition on its cultivation and use. In Nazi Germany, the film *Jud Süss* portrayed a despicable Jew, reinforcing the stereotype that was used to justify the Final Solution, and *The Triumph of Will* served as a call to arms for the Third Reich. On the Allied side, Frank Capra directed a series of propaganda films called *Why We Fight*. The newsreels that used to be shown before the feature at movie theaters in my youth sometimes had a propagandistic take on world events.

One reason for going to the movies used to be that it was an ad-free entertainment alternative to network TV. But over the years it has become the norm to have to watch five to ten minutes of commercial advertisements before the theater shows trailers, which are another kind of advertising. Trailers can be entertaining, but any trailer for a movie that I have no interest in seeing is noise. Those of us who sit there waiting for the movie to start are a captive audience.

Some premovie ads are demographically targeted to the audience. I'm a military veteran and have no problem per se with ads promoting military service; but I have a problem with the glorification of war in the media. I've noticed that propagandistic military recruitment ads are often shown before action films that mainly appeal to young males, ads that glorify military service and portray war as an adventure. Such propaganda has been used throughout the modern era to recruit soldiers. This is just the latest slick Hollywood version.

Another encroachment of advertising in the cinema experience is product placement. Many movies are partially underwritten by revenue from advertisers who pay for their product to be featured prominently in the film. It's not exactly subliminal advertising, but it's close, in that it's intended to create a positive association between the product and elements of the film with which viewers are meant to identify.

Just as some cartoons on TV are essentially advertisements for lines of toys, now we have blockbuster movies based on those franchised, trademarked toys. Many adults, it appears, enjoy watching giant fighting robots and the fantastic exploits of superheroes. But while we're being entertained, we're also being pitched, perhaps for gifts for our children or grandchildren, or the tie-in video game or graphic novel. This is another example of how culture is no longer a grassroots, bottom-up phenomenon, but is fed to us by the mass media, top-down. Does anyone still play marbles or hopscotch?

Signs and Billboards

Some signage is necessary to direct people in the right direction, but the ubiquity of commercial signs, posters, and billboards competing for our attention is a major form of pollution in the mental environment. We've become accustomed to seeing signs all over the place. They just keep getting bigger and, with the advent of huge digital billboards, more attention-grabbing. Advertising technology that you used to only see in places like Times Square is now being used in every American city and maybe even your neighborhood.

Only the blind can escape the onslaught of giant print and arresting visuals. Huge billboards can be a visual blight, crowding us with competing messages in urban environments and obscuring the scenery in natural environments. Digital billboards with their rotating sequence of messages present a distraction to drivers. They exist to attract our attention—made you look—and are one more source of noise in our lives.

Attempts by neighborhood associations and citizens groups to limit the size, number, and locations of billboards are frequently countered by trade groups with big budgets that lobby city and county councils and state legislatures. In Columbia, South Carolina, a recent bill proposed that advertisers should be reimbursed for "lost revenue" if billboards were banned. I don't know if the bill passed.

Industry lawyers argue in court that advertising is free speech, protected by the First Amendment to the Constitution; and they're right. No distinction is made between commercial messages, even if they're blatantly deceitful or eyesores and other forms of free speech.

During the weeks leading up to elections, political signs pop up like mushrooms in the rainy season. They litter the streets and the lawns of our neighbors. They compete for our attention, urging us to vote yes or no, to vote for this or that candidate. Unfortunately, unlike mushrooms, they're not biodegradable and often remain a blight on the land long after the elections are over. Waste. Noise.

The American flag is used by many businesses to influence public perception and attract customers. You may have seen the arms race effect in your own community, in which rival car dealers compete to fly the biggest flag, in an attempt to appear more patriotic. The biggest American flags I've ever seen have flown over car dealerships.

Television

By the Numbers

As a member of the first generation to grow up with TV—and to remember what it was like before most homes had a TV set—I can see the impact the medium has had on our society. Commercial TV provides instant infotainment "by the numbers."

The sale of commercial time to sponsors drives everything on the broadcast networks and commercial cable networks, from the schedule to decisions about the content. The cost of a given advertising spot on a given channel at a given time is determined by supply and demand, as evidenced by the show's "numbers," usually Nielsen ratings. Nielsen Media Research provides the numbers by conducting national surveys of viewing habits, and smaller surveys in local markets.

I may tune in to see the weekend network evening news broadcast, only to find that it has been preempted by a sporting event. That's because the network knows it can charge more for the latter, because more people watch sports than watch the news. If a sporting event runs past the time allotted on the schedule, the rest of the evening's programming is likely to be pushed back. By the numbers.

On a recent Sunday, I tuned in to the 6:00 p.m. news on ABC, only to find it preempted by a basketball game. When I turned to NBC at 6:30 p.m., that newscast had been preempted by golf, or rather a long pause at a golf tournament. Apparently play had been stopped for over an hour, due to rain, and it didn't look like it would resume anytime soon. But instead of broadcasting the news, NBC filled up the time with replays and commentary, presumably for the increased advertising revenue. In effect, NBC decided that golf replays were more important than the news.

Programming

When we watch commercial TV, not a minute goes by without something being pitched to us. We used to be able to watch programs on an uncluttered screen. Nowadays, at the very least, there's a network logo at the bottom of the screen, and often there are ads for upcoming shows.

The formulaic plot structures of sitcoms and dramatic series are utterly predictable, with commercial time programmed between uniformly timed "acts." The problem introduced in the first act surely will be resolved in the last act, just before the final credits roll. Most shows are either thirty or sixty minutes long (including commercials), never thirty-four or sixty-seven—except on premium channels—and you always know just when the climax will occur. For the most part, next week's episode will be pretty much like this week's episode.

An hour-long program on commercial TV contains far less than an hour of program content. In the 1960s, the program-to-ad ratio in prime time was approximately fifty-one minutes of program content in a sixty-minute program. Today, it is more like forty-two minutes. A typical half-hour program in prime time these days has twenty-two minutes of content, six minutes of national ads, and two minutes of local ads.

A show's time slot may be shuffled around, so network officials can see how its numbers fare in this or that slot, relative to the competing channels. Quality of programming takes a backseat to the program's numbers and the consequent worth of the commercial spots. Whether a new series continues or is cancelled may depend on how it fares against the competition in that time slot, this month. For the most part, advertising revenue determines a show's longevity on the air.

To cultivate a base of loyal viewers who will keep the numbers for a given program/series high over time, TV producers create memorable fictional characters—Matt Dillon and Miss Kitty, Perry Mason, Fonzie, Columbo, Archie and Edith Bunker, Seinfeld, Monk, Jack Bauer, etc.—and feature/create celebrities—Oprah, Regis, Judge Judy, Dr. Oz, Dr. Phil, etc.—with whom viewers will identify, form faux relationships, and want to follow over time, as if they were personal friends. This attempt to create the illusion of a relationship also extends to news broadcasts, during which anchors thank you for tuning in and "hope to see you again tomorrow," as if they know and care when you're watching. This practice is so pervasive it is invisible to most viewers. It may seem innocuous, but it's part of the social engineering strategy of the advertising establishment and a staple of misrepresentation in our propaganda society.

If commercial television is largely a wasteland of imitative premises, formulaic plots, and predictable character portrayals, it is due to the numbers. Humor and drama on network TV are homogenized and aimed at the largest common denominator; it is different in the film industry or on premium TV channels, where stories are more likely to have a beginning, a middle, and an end rather than year after year of new episodes of the same old stuff.

In the early years of TV, there were anthology series like *Science Fiction Theater, Alfred Hitchcock, Twilight Zone,* and *Playhouse 90,* but anthologies didn't keep viewers coming back the way series with familiar, predictable characters did. When I heard about the innovative plot structure of the series *24*, I naively thought that it was an anthology vehicle that would follow a protagonist over twenty-four hours, with the possibility that he or she may die, as would happen in a movie. I thought that the next season would feature a new protagonist, a new storyline. But no, Jack Bauer proved to be marketable, and lasted for many seasons with almost-identical story arcs.

The critical and popular success of HBO, Showtime, and other pay channels proves that an emphasis on quality and originality can generate a profit. Before the advent of HBO, the networks mounted a campaign against "pay TV," using images of viewers inserting coins into slots on their TVs in order to watch. The commercial TV conglomerate didn't want an alternate model of programming or any competition that would lower their ratings. The popularity of premium pay channels suggests that television could have evolved in a very different manner in the 1950s had it not been immediately appropriated by merchandisers.

With few exceptions, programming on the commercial channels continues to be numbers driven, resulting in the proliferation of so-called reality shows. These programs present artificially contrived situations as "reality," often encouraging cast members to be shallow, deceitful, and exploitive in order to win the game at hand. Real-life manufactured melodrama provides catharsis or vicarious thrills, is cheap relative to scripted dramatic series, and moves merchandise. Reality shows have proven so popular, untold thousands of viewers long for the fame associated with appearing in such a show. They are willing to let themselves be exploited, humiliated, and emotionally manipulated for the entertainment of the audience.

Clone cop shows depict increasingly detailed violence, clone sitcoms compete for the deepest cleavage and the edgiest sexual innuendoes, and clone reality shows aim for new depths of betrayal and selfishness and degradation, all in the name of entertainment. It's an unending downward spiral of the mediocre and the superficial and the trendy that—Hobson's choice—they tell us we chose. "We're only giving them what they want," say the network executives. By the numbers.

Adspeak

Commercials for products and services depict events that seem to occur in parallel universes resembling our own, where perky people hold up boxes of a product and sing its praises by name, or assure viewers that a product or service has improved their lives in some manner we can identify with. The actors mimic actual human behavior but often don't seem real to me. Commercials frequently set up a straw dog—gray hair, dandruff, halitosis, water spots on glasses—and demolish it within a fifteen-second to one-minute dramatic pitch for a product we didn't know we needed. (See appendix 2, "100 Things You Learn on TV.")

The manufacturers of Dr. Scholl's orthotic insoles (footpads) would like us to believe everyone needs their product. To that end, they tell us to get our feet mapped on a gizmo at a local "foot-mapping center," to get our number—because everyone has a number, and we all need footpads. They make it sound scientific, without ever making that claim, and one footpad enthusiast calls out, "I feel energized!" The everyman satisfied customer in the ad says, "I'm a believer!" and the manufacturer wants you to be a believer too.

There is a series of ads in which an everyman character agrees to "prove" that Aleve is the best pain medication by using a rival brand for a day. The ads then show the person cringing or grimacing with pain as he attends to daily tasks. Unable to endure his pain until the end of the day, he asks plaintively, "Can I have my Aleve back now?" Then he asserts, "For my pain, I want my Aleve!" The implied message is that Aleve is the best choice for you too.

News by the Numbers

In an ideal democratic nation, the press would be truly free, with content unaffected by commercial considerations or profit motive. TV news isn't what it used to be. In my lifetime I've seen it change radically. Walter Cronkite was probably the most trusted TV journalist of his generation, but I always chafed at his arrogant presumption in proclaiming at the end of each broadcast, "And that's the way it is." According to whom? According to the trusted Uncle Walter.

Just as TV sitcoms and dramas present sympathetic characters with whom viewers feel they have a relationship, TV news has its celebrity anchors and reporters, many of whom imply in their sign-offs that they have a two-way relationship with you, the viewer. Brian Williams says, "Thank you for being here with us. Of course, we hope to see you right back here tomorrow night!" Scott Pelley and David Muir also perpetuate the lie, saying they'll "see you" on a later broadcast, and a CNN anchor tells you he's "so glad to have your company." The lie of the reciprocal relationship is also perpetuated on local news broadcasts. These deceptive sign-offs are such a cliché that they're invisible to most viewers. But they're used pervasively because they work; they promote viewer loyalty and tend to increase market share.

The movie *Network*, with its brilliant script by Paddy Chayefsky, made the clear point that the network news we watch is presented by attractive, likeable rich people who tell us what their even richer bosses want us to know or think. I hoped at the time I first saw it that its spot-on satire might serve as a prophylactic against such pernicious programming, but it proved to be merely predictive of the current news circus. I can't imagine hearing the word "plutocracy" issuing from the mouth of Brian Williams, Scott Pelley, Anderson Cooper, or any other news anchor. Their bosses wouldn't allow it. Many or most Americans probably don't know what plutocracy means, and that's the way the owners of the mass media want it.

Infotainment

The progressive blurring of the lines between news and entertainment and between factual reporting and opinion mongering is a result of the advertising-driven ratings system. Starting in the early days of cable TV, I became a regular viewer of *CNN Headline News*. In the morning it provided me with an alternative to *Today* and *Good Morning America*, which I labeled "chatty news," featuring everybody's celebrity news buddies. *Headline News* was originally mostly newsreaders and video, presenting an overview of national and world news, with the last five minutes of each half hour devoted to sports and celebrities. I sometimes watched CNN too, and was thankful to have 24/7 TV news coverage available. Ted Turner was a media hero to me.

The first stage of my disillusionment with *CNN Headline News* came when Time, Inc. bought CNN from Ted Turner and the standards immediately fell. It increasingly began to compete for a higher Nielsen share by becoming chattier, offering more popular hot topics and cool video clips, and less hard news. Still, I continued to watch it for years because I couldn't stomach the morning news alternatives on the broadcast networks. I watched the progressive decline in hard news coverage and its replacement by chatty news, and Robin Meade greeting her morning audience with her signature, "Good morning, sunshine!"

It used to be that the original three broadcast networks offered straight-up news reporting—one or more anchors seated at a desk, reports from correspondents, and footage of events. The news division might not have been as profitable as other divisions, but it was given some slack, as a reputation for quality news programming was a matter of prestige. However, the boundary between news and entertainment has become blurred, both locally and nationally, and we progressively get more coverage of entertaining trivialities and ephemera, at the expense of comprehensive coverage of important news stories.

Today and *Good Morning America* changed the morning network news by relying on pleasant visages and perky personalities and chat. Chatty news has become the norm for local news broadcasts, whatever time of day. Apparently most viewers like the format, because it's designed to make you feel like you have a personal relationship with the nice people on your screen. They tell you what's happening, are always glad to see you, and hope you'll tune in again the next day. It's all a formula driven by the numbers, and how many people tune in seems to be more important than the quality of the news reporting.

Headline News gradually changed its focus from a roundup of news stories to tabloid journalism, with excessive coverage of the sensational story of the week. Coverage of the latest celebrity death or trial of a mother accused of killing her child dominates the broadcasts—and, by the way, millions are still starving in Somalia. A more honest moniker for the network would have been Headline News and Entertainment. By the time the network changed its name to HLN, I was ready to move on. These days I watch CNN when I need a morning news fix, but it's still too chatty for me, and I miss Ted Turner's pioneering version of a 24/7 strictly news network. Al Jazeera America is off to a good start, and I hope its "straight news" format doesn't succumb to market forces. Democracy can't survive on a diet of propaganda and infotainment.

Local anchors, newsreaders, and reporters either present themselves as "your news team," there to serve you, or as part of your family. They're chatty, they joke with one another, and they preface news items with personal comments like "As a father myself ..." Mini-ads assure that local news anchors are "on your side," no matter who you are. What passes for news today can include teasers ("More at eleven!"), trailers for upcoming specials or documentaries, an amusing viral video clip of the day, and items about neighbors helping neighbors. The program is designed to make you feel good inside and want to tune in again the next day for more of the same. It is news designed by the numbers.

Ratings-driven news isn't free from advertiser influence. The airwaves are controlled by corporations—everything has to make a profit—and so the networks compete with each other by hiring the most attractive and likable news people. Just as Paddy Chayefsky predicted in *Network*, we're getting infotained by the folks who are supposed to be informing us. We also get subtle product placements with our news. NBC has a tie-in with the Weather Channel, which has a tie-in with L.L.Bean, whose logo is visible on the rain gear of the Weather Channel staff who appear on NBC News.

And then there are the talking heads, like Rush Limbaugh and Glenn Beck, who get paid for saying anything that comes into their heads. Their job is to blur the line between opinion and fact and to ignite emotional responses. Fox News discovered that there was money to be made when it shifted from a news format to a propaganda format. And Fox really blurred the line between opinion and fact by touting its biased news coverage as "fair and balanced."

"Conservatives will almost always defend Fox's claim," writes conservative Richard Viguerie (2004, 229) "... but they find it hard to do so without a smirk or a smile on their faces." Fox News has cultivated a knee-jerk conservative following that regards their programming from the following point of view: "Finally, a news channel that tells the truth, unlike the liberal media." It's the Fox News brand.

Energy Advertising

Political agendas can be indirectly served by industry advertising campaigns that utilize the techniques of propaganda to influence voters in ways that benefit the industry. From my observations over the years, the energy industry is most likely to use slick television propaganda to mold public opinion—oil and gas, coal, and in the past, nuclear energy. Some ads have been cute, clever animations: an everyman icon rescued from scary scarcity by the hot air balloon of nuclear energy, with a carefully constructed voiceover that makes the energy option seem like a no-brainer. Whether for animated commercials or those featuring an attractive spokesperson and arresting visuals, the voiceover follows the same propaganda formula, designed to persuade in the guise of informing.

A recent example is a series of ads by the American Petroleum Institute (API) featuring a perky blonde spokeswoman who asks and answers questions about America's energy future. I missed a few words in my transcription efforts of one of the earlier ads, but what follows is almost verbatim:

> Question: How do we grow our economy, increase energy security, and create one million new American jobs?
>
> Answer: Safely develop oil and natural gas right here by expanding access onshore and off ... develop Canadian oil sands ... tapping more than a century's worth of natural gas. All that could put a million more Americans to work. Good news? Without question. Log on to [the API website] EnergyTomorrow.org to learn more.

Case closed. No need to worry. We know what we're doing, and it's all for your benefit.

The intent is to get the viewer to feel good about the interests served by API and to believe that everything the institute does is smart, safe, and benign. Only positive things are said about the industries represented; nothing is said about potential risks to the environment. "Safely" implies that only methods *proven* safe will be used to ensure America's energy future. Trust us.

"One million new American jobs" is a nice, round, reassuring number, but who arrived at that figure, and how? "Good news ... without question" tells viewers not to question what they've just heard.

Here is the verbatim ad copy to another ad in this series, which shows the pretty spokeswoman connecting dots on a rapidly changing computer screen:

> What connects the dots between new jobs, cleaner air, a manufacturing renaissance, and energy security?
>
> American natural gas. The fact is, America is now the world's number one natural gas producer, thanks to safe, proven hydraulic fracturing technology, making clean-burning domestic natural gas the fuel of choice. From advanced technology to a reenergized American economy, natural gas connects them all.

This state-of-the-art ad has many of the classic elements of effective propaganda, from its clever ad copy and its card-stacked ideas to its juxtaposition of visual images and metaphors, shown in rapid succession, amplifying the effect of the carefully scripted words. The confident spokeswoman walks through a computer-animated environment, pointing things out as she walks the blue line that connects the blue dots. One of the blue dots levitates and becomes a computer-animated image of a clean-burning natural gas stove burner.

Some of the words she says—for example, "number-one natural gas producer"—appear in giant block letters behind her. Other words are amplified by quick live or animated scenes or images: a cluster of working people, a pristine nature scene with butterfly, a happy family whose daughter blows out candles on her birthday cake, workers on the floor of an industrial plant. When the spokeswoman says "safe, proven hydraulic fracturing technology," we see an animation that illustrates that the fracking occurs deep below the water table and that layers of cement and steel separate the natural gas from the dirt and rock—as if that means it's safe.

This bombardment of auditory and visual information is packed into a thirty-second spot. Again, you are referred to the API website to "learn more," but if you check it out, you'll only learn more about what they want you to learn. The ad uses cherry picking and card stacking, characterizing fracking as "safe, proven," as if these were absolute terms, implying that there's no downside. I have no doubt that the industry has contingency plans should something related to fracking go terribly wrong. But I don't expect that the API will volunteer to reveal these plans, because to admit their existence would be to admit that a risk exists. That would be information.

There are legitimate concerns about hydraulic fracturing, exploiting oil sands, constructing a Canada-to-Mexico pipeline, and expanded offshore drilling. The natural gas industry doesn't want to reveal all the chemicals it uses in fracking or to admit there's any risk the water supply may be contaminated. The ads imply that government regulation isn't needed; offshore oil spills happen, but all future drilling will be safe.

Other ads by the energy industry suggest there's such a thing as "clean coal," depicting beleaguered Americans in a boxing ring or a rodeo, staggering but buoyed by America's energy future. Another ad by the API uses the same Q&A format as above, asking "Do you own an oil company?" It suggests that anyone invested in mutual funds or an IRA, etc., "owns" an oil company and presumably should be sympathetic to the interests of the petroleum industry.

Tobacco Advertising

The energy industry campaign to downplay the role hydrocarbon emissions play in climate change reminds me of the media campaign to downplay the health risks of tobacco smoking. Advertising has long been used to promote smoking and other public health hazards. Let's consider Uncle Louie, who smoked two packs a day from age seventeen to age sixty, when he died from chronic obstructive pulmonary disease.

Sure, he kept smoking despite his progressive respiratory problems, but can we simply conclude that he's fully responsible for years of foolish behavior? As I understand the legal concept of limited liability, we need to understand that—to a certain degree—Uncle Louie was a victim of misleading advertising engineered by highly intelligent and highly paid professionals, whose field of expertise was the deception of the public. Louie also saw a lot of attractive people smoking on TV.

Perhaps he was influenced by ads for Lucky Strikes that said, "Light a Lucky and you'll never miss sweets that make you fat," or ads that asserted that because Luckies were "toasted" there was "no throat irritation, no cough." Or maybe he was reassured by endorsements for Camel cigarettes by such celebrities as John Wayne, or by the ads that said, "According to repeated nationwide surveys, more doctors smoke Camels than any other cigarette."

In the early years of TV, I noticed a lot more celebrity endorsements than I do today, mostly from TV and movie stars. Some shows were sponsored by one product, and it wasn't unusual to see ads for cigarettes and other products featuring the star(s) of the show. Lucille Ball and Desi Arnaz pitched Phillip Morris cigarettes, Jack Benny endorsed Lucky Strikes, and James Arness and Amanda Blake (in costume as Matt Dillon and Miss Kitty from *Gunsmoke*) promoted L&Ms. Celebrities who endorsed Camels included Tony Curtis, Maureen O'Hara, Alan Ladd, and Charlton Heston. Even the Flintstones appeared in ads, puffing away on Winstons.

Many cigarette brands used gimmicks, jingles, and slogans in their TV ads. Raleighs and Belairs (a menthol cigarette) had coupons that could be redeemed for merchandise on every pack. Cigarettes were described as "a breath of fresh air." Some of the slogans were, "Breathe easy, smoke clean with Belair ... It just makes good sense to smoke Raleighs ... Smoke twice as refreshed." In one ad, a pretty woman said, "I don't see why *everybody* doesn't smoke Raleighs!"

Everybody from my generation knows what LSMFT means: Lucky Strike means fine tobacco. "It's time right now," one ad said, "for a Lucky Strike!" Another one played on the common expression "happy-go-lucky" and turned it into the slogan, "Be happy, go Lucky!"

Perhaps the most famous TV cigarette campaign featured the Marlboro Man and Marlboro Country. It was geared to attract male smokers who identified with rugged cowboys, ridin' and ropin' out on the range, but some of the ads admitted that "ladies ... like them too!" The jingles were "You get a lot to like with a Marlboro: filter, flavor, flip-top box." and "Where there's a man, there's a Marlboro!" The Marlboro Country ads featured the thundering theme from *The Magnificent Seven*. "Come to where the flavor is," one ad invited, "Come to Marlboro Country!" A series of Marlboro Man ads asked "What kind of man is he?" and depicted rugged outdoorsmen: fishermen, white water rafters, mountain climbers, bow-and-arrow hunters. Some Marlboro ads claimed "lower tar and nicotine" but never specified lower than what.

Newport promised "the smoothest-tasting menthol cigarette ... never harsh, never rough." Viceroy ads sometimes featured cowboys, but the copy was always about taste. "Don't settle for some of the taste, some of the time ... the taste that's right ... the good taste never quits!" Pall Mall assured that its cigarettes were "outstanding, and they are mild." Ads claimed that the "nose, throat, and accessory organs" weren't adversely affected by smoking Chesterfields. Winstons were said to taste good, "like a cigarette should," and the black-eye-sporting actors in Tareyton ads told us they'd "rather fight than switch."

Celebrity Endorsements

Cigarettes weren't the only products pitched by celebrities during the early years of TV. Jack Benny endorsed Texaco, John Wayne appeared in ads for Gillette, Dinah Shore sang the praises of Chevy, Ronald Reagan sold Borax soap, Groucho Marx pitched for De Soto, and the Monkees did ads for Kool-Aid. The children's market also had its celebrity ads. The Lone Ranger and Rocky and Bullwinkle endorsed Cheerios. Captain Midnight pitched for Ovaltine, and invited kids to join the Secret Squadron and order a secret decoder ring. Roy Rogers promoted a toy trick-shooter hat with a spring-loaded concealed gun, although he was a white-hatted hero who never would have resorted to such sneaky tricks.

Celebrity endorsements aren't as common on TV in the United States as they once were, although some major movie stars who don't appear in commercials in America do endorse products in foreign TV markets. The few movie stars who do commercial endorsements in prime time these days are mostly older males, known for their deep voices and gravitas: James Earl Jones, Tommy Lee Jones, Fred Thompson, and Samuel L. Jackson. The few female celebrities who endorse products on prime time TV are attractive older actresses.

Radio

The only radio station I routinely listen to is the local NPR station. I seldom listen to commercial radio, unless I'm a captive audience in a waiting room. But I've listened to enough over the years to know that, like TV, radio programming is largely determined by advertising. Radio stations tend to be more specialized than the broadcast TV networks, aiming to attract listeners in distinct niche markets, from news/talk radio to a wide variety of musical styles—rock (hard, lite, golden oldies, alternative), gospel, rhythm & blues, rap, religious, country & western, jazz and classical. Many stations have gone through a series of incarnations, their management studying the market and the competition and adopting the most profitable format. Country music stations now predominate, with news/talk stations coming in second (Deitz n.d.).

Having sampled some popular local FM stations by way of research, here's what I've learned: the rock/pop/country stations all have similar formats, with forty to forty-five minutes per hour of music and fifteen to twenty minutes of advertising and station identification/promotion. Some stations have snippets of news and weather and traffic reports and such, but it's mostly ten to twenty minutes of song after song, then a six- to seven-minute barrage of ads for everything from car dealerships and big box stores to senior living referral services and strip clubs. The tropes of commercial radio haven't changed from the days when I used to listen regularly: enthusiastic hard sell, rapid patter, corny promotional skits performed by actors with precise diction and inflections, jingles that include phone numbers, and claims that you'll never get a better deal than you will *today* or find a lower price *anywhere*.

What's changed? For one thing, political punditry has become a staple of talk radio, and Rush Limbaugh has admitted that he makes a living from delivering an audience to advertisers. He's credible to his core audience because he strokes their prejudices, and he's just the most visible of this new breed of propagandists. There are radio pundits who are popular enough to make a good living for themselves by becoming spokespersons for this or that conspiracy theory or political advocacy movement.

I remember when National Public Radio was truly commercial free and only promoted station programming. Now NPR programs are sponsored, and although broadcasts aren't riddled with ads throughout, you'll hear brief ads at the top of the hour. If you think NPR has a tree-hugging bias, it's not reflected in the sponsorships. Among the websites advertised on *All Things Considered* is thinkaboutit.org, one of the API's PR sites.

The other change is that commercial radio has become a major platform—second only to TV—for political advertising. Just as Christmas-season sales are responsible for a large percentage of the annual profit of a lot of stores, election-season ad sales are predictably responsible for high profits in the radio business. Even those nonpartisan stations benefit from the cyclical sale of political advertising. Most countries in the European Union, including the United Kingdom, don't allow paid political ads on TV or radio because of the unfair influence of Big Money on political campaigns, but the sale of political ads in the United States is largely unregulated in those markets.

I love many kinds of music, but the main reason I don't listen to more of it on the radio is the signal to noise ratio. You can hear new songs or enjoy old favorites for free on commercial radio, but that doesn't mean you don't pay a price, when you're bombarded with ads—many of them for products and services you do not want. More noise.

The Top 40 has been around for a long time, and most commercial radio stations have standardized playlists, whatever the featured genre. The playlists are carefully crafted to grab maximum market share. If they reflect the tastes of the target audience, they also help to shape them. In this way, commercial radio plays a role in the homogenization of popular culture.

The Internet

While I appreciate and enjoy the wealth of information and entertainment that is so easily accessible online, it's often a quid pro quo proposition, in which I have to accept exposure to ads in order to access content. I wish I could pay a fee and do my surfing ad free, but that will not happen. I understand that the revenue stream from ads makes a lot of content possible, but this is yet another instance where we are commodities, a captive audience delivered to advertisers.

The *State* newspaper used to print the movie schedule daily. Now it makes additional advertising money for providing this information. You have to go to its website, where you will be exposed to multiple ads as you search for the movie times at local theaters. This is just one example of the kind of information you used to find in print and now have to search for online, on ad-laden pages.

Every time I log on to my e-mail, I see rotating ads on the page. There are also ads in the margins of my inbox, such as, "Satisfy your curiosity. Run a background check on anyone online in seconds." Some of the ads on my log-on page are for brand-name products, store chains, or Publishers Clearing House giveaways. But others have teasers designed to get you to click, like ads that hype some "ridiculously easy trick that __________ doesn't want you to know about" or "the food you should *never* eat" or tell you to "eat this and never diet again." Some teaser ads appear political, inviting you to rate the president, or show the famous picture of Michelle Obama giving Carla Bruni the stink eye and inviting you to click and find out why.

I seldom click, but did check out an ad that comes around from time to time: "The End of Barack Obama." An alternate teaser is "this story could bring the worst shame to the White House since the Clinton era." These turn out to be incendiary advertisements by Stansberry Research. They purport to be about a "scandal" that will be the downfall of the Obama administration, although they appear to be about an identified piece of legislation, not a scandal. I tuned out after listening to several minutes of Mr. Stansberry going on and on about a video he'd eventually get around to showing, a video that he says will prove all his claims. He first assures us that he has a track record of accurate predictions, then goes on to predict an imminent stock market crash due to government regulation, and promotes his plan to avoid the dire consequences of the impending catastrophe. He predicts that governments will shut down, banks will close, martial law will be declared, and the economy will experience "the biggest financial crash in fifty years."

It seems that anyone who can afford it can get his or her message in front of me whenever I check my e-mail, whether it is someone with a legitimate business or someone with an alarmist message. As with commercial TV, you get content for free, but not without a price.

Data mining has become a big business, and the consumer is the commodity. According to Frank Pasquale in an October 17, 2014, *New York Times* article, "The Dark Market for Personal Data," there are approximately four thousand data brokers, and it is a $156 billion a year industry. While there are legitimate concerns about government surveillance, it appears that security agencies are more focused on pinpointing potential terrorists than on snooping on average citizens. Not so with the business sector, whose "intelligence gathering" activities have a distinct and profitable purpose, which is to study and classify individual consumers and then to sell the data to marketers. Your name can end up on a list because you are believed, rightly or wrongly, to have Alzheimer's disease or a criminal record, or because you order a lot of books on gardening.

Data miners get their information not just from the Internet but from loyalty-card data from retailers, magazine subscription lists, and public records, among other sources. They know you well enough to target you for specific advertisements on informational, commercial, and social media sites. You're the subject of scrutiny when you surf the Internet and share information online. Most people don't bother to read the details of the "terms of use" agreements when they click "I Agree" in order to use a site, but they often waive their privacy rights when they do. Facebook is free because it compiles data on its users' circumstances, interests, and preferences to sell to advertisers.

It may be convenient to find advertisements and recommendations for products you're interested in when you shop online, but it means that the data analysts know a lot about your habits and preferences. We haven't gotten to the point where our TVs watch us back, as Orwell described in *1984*, but our computers and other Internet platforms are interactive, and you can be sure that Big Brother (in his business suit) is "watching" and studying you.

Industrial Propaganda

If you do what the API's TV ads suggest and check out EnergyTomorrow.org, you find a public relations website with links to affiliated sites. You learn that the API is the national trade association for all things petroleum-related, and that it represents more than 490 corporate members. No wonder it can afford to bombard us daily with slick, feel-good ads, whose primary purpose appears to be to persuade us to trust the petroleum industry.

Local energy providers also try to reassure us that the means they use to provide energy are safe, as if that were an absolute guarantee. Sometimes when I log onto my newspaper's website, I see an ad from Westinghouse, showing steam coming from the tower of a state nuclear plant, with the caption, "It's just steam. And lots of clean electricity." There is no mention of radioactive fuel that will remain toxic for thousands of years or the risks of a catastrophic accident. It's just steam.

If I taught a college course on propaganda, I could give a lecture on adspeak and PR phrasings and illogic, using the Energy Tomorrow site and its affiliates as my sources. The material online presents terms such as "America's Energy Future" and "increasing energy security" as if they were trademarked and new, nice-sounding phrases such as "investing in the promise of America." Then we're introduced to "America's New Energy Future: The Unconventional Oil and Gas Revolution," which perhaps is going on beneath your feet. But, not to worry: "safety is our first priority." Not profits, safety. Trust us.

You won't find the word *risk* in the description of the industry's unconventional and unspecified efforts to extract oil from the earth, let alone a discussion of a risk/benefits ratio for any given unconventional technology. What you'll find is that "unconventional oil and gas activity is already revolutionizing America's energy future" and that it is "an important engine for job creation." Who knew?

You also won't find facts and figures to back up claims of

the million jobs and billions of dollars in tax receipts that the unconventional oil and gas revolution will generate or any timeline indicating when these benefits will kick in. Trust us.

At the bottom of Energy Tomorrow's homepage are links to blogs, with headlines such as "Keystone XL: Safe for Our Country" and "Stepping Forward on Offshore Drilling." This website purports to provide information to those whose curiosity has been piqued by the TV ads, but if you want objective information about the risks of fracking, offshore drilling, or the Keystone pipeline, this is not the place to go. The text on the homepage even tries to recruit citizen advocates for the API, suggesting "together, we can find solutions" and providing a link for us to "get involved" with this propaganda campaign.

An affiliate site, Who Owns Big Oil?, expands on the TV ad that asks, "Do you own an oil company?" It suggests, "chances are you do." In a leap of illogic, it equates having a tiny stake in the oil industry via pensions and mutual funds, etc., with "owning" an oil company. Presumably, that notion will make me sympathize with "unlocking" reserves of oil and gas by "unconventional" means. Trust us.

Energy Answered, another affiliate site, uses a Q&A format to discuss oil sands and fracking: How important are oil sands to America's energy future? Will China purchase Canada's oil sands crude if the Keystone pipeline isn't built? How does hydraulic fracturing work?

According to the website, fracking is "a safe and well-regulated technology that has been used for more than sixty years in more than a million wells." Current estimates project somewhere around thirty-five thousand new wells per year. Who knew? According to Energy Answered, fracking will increase our energy security and "improve our ability to generate electricity, heat homes, and power vehicles for generations to come." If there's a downside to fracking, you won't read about it here. We're told that the fluids, or lubricating chemicals, used in fracking are "a mix of common industrial and household materials" and that hydraulic fracturing wells "go far below underground aquifers." We're assured that wells have steel and concrete shielding to protect groundwater and that "additional protection is offered by the impermeable rock formations that lie between the oil and natural gas formations and the groundwater."

"Impermeable" sounds reassuring, but is it accurate? What the website doesn't mention is the risk associated with the extensive shattering of natural rock formations by underground explosions and the storage of massive amounts of waste water far below ground, year after year. It doesn't mention that, according to the National Research Council and the US Geological Survey, fracking and other petroleum extraction technologies can cause minor earthquakes.

Nobody knows the long-term geological effects that may result from continued reliance on fracking, and if the API has its way, we're just getting started. According to Energy Answered, Canadian oil sands currently account for "more than a million barrels per day of US oil imports, a figure that could reach five million barrels per day in 2030 with full oil sands development."

Since the API ads don't push products or services to individual consumers, their purpose appears to be to promote good feelings about the petroleum industry and to reassure the public that everything it does is safe. Some of their ads prior to the last presidential election invited viewers to become "energy voters," presumably to elect politicians who trust the petroleum industry to regulate itself and to expand the use of unconventional petroleum extraction technologies. When the ads invite you to "learn more at EnergyTomorrow.org," they aren't offering a source of objective information. The websites exist to persuade you, while making you think you are well informed. That's what effective public relations is all about.

Issue Propaganda

No matter what your bias may be or what cause you advocate, there's a propaganda website for you. White supremacists use the same techniques as Muslim jihadists. They're there to stroke your prejudices, influence you in the guise of informing you, and possibly recruit you. Propaganda sites can be sponsored by corporations or affinity groups or terrorist organizations. Their goals are to make you feel that you belong to a group of like-minded people, or to win you over, perhaps to the point of making a commitment to action.

In recent months we've seen a surge in growth by the Islamic State in Syria (ISIS), fueled by slick, sophisticated online propaganda. ISIS has mounted a worldwide recruitment campaign, using images of brutality and the lure of martyrdom (as a ticket to paradise) to lure new recruits. The ISIS brand appears to consist of black flags with white script, concealed faces, and beheadings.

The Internet also makes it easy for people to disseminate whatever lies or propagandistic screeds represent their beliefs, via e-mail. There are people who believe that something must be true if it appears in print, and they don't hesitate to forward it to everyone on their e-mail lists. Propagandists thrive in an open environment where opinions and lies can be presented as facts to true believers and potential converts.

Part 2: Cultural Changes

Sports

Commercial advertising on TV has shaped many sports, none more than professional football. (Indeed, live soccer wasn't available to US fans for many years, because the continuous play isn't conducive to advertising breaks.) The best players have always been well compensated, but advertising has transformed sports into a highly lucrative business. Today, aspiring sports stars expect to become fabulously wealthy. Superstar athletes attain the status of media demigods.

The commercial transformation of football started in 1970, when ABC broke away from the tradition of weekend games with *Monday Night Football*. With innovations like color, more cameras, and slow-motion replays, it got good ratings and became a TV staple. Now millions of new dollars in ad revenues and exclusive TV contracts were available to teams and leagues. Salaries for players and coaches soared. And today we have Thursday and Saturday night NFL games too. Since the first Super Bowl in 1967, the event has become an annual extravaganza, with an estimated 112 million viewers. A thirty-second Super Bowl ad costs millions of dollars.

The National Collegiate Athletic Association (NCAA) now generates approximately $11 billion a year from advertising, changing the face of collegiate athletics. Only a few college sports programs generate revenue for their schools, but those that do can produce millions in profits. Talented student athletes become commodities. Ideally, athletic scholarships are intended to allow athletes to get a college education, and the NCAA set standards for academic performance that had to be met for a student athlete to play on a team. It was recently revealed that for many years the University of North Carolina (UNC) had allowed some of its athletes to get credit for bogus courses, so that they could play (Wolken 2014). If a prestigious institution like UNC found a way around NCAA rules, it's likely other schools have too. This scandal has revived the discussion about whether athletes on profitable college teams should be considered students or employees.

Only a tiny fraction of college athletes will ever go on to careers in professional sports. Therefore, a quality education should be the primary goal of sports scholarships, but clearly some student athletes are cheated in this regard. According to an article by Armstrong Williams (2014), star athletes "are owned by the NCAA and the universities they attend." Their names and likenesses can be used for profit by the NCAA and the schools, but the athletes don't make a cent. During their college careers, they risk sustaining injuries such as concussions that may carry long-term consequences. Head coaches in money-generating programs make six- and seven-figure salaries, while the team members are considered amateurs.

Some fans would hate to see this tradition change, but it is not fair to exploit student athletes, many of whom put their bodies on the line in hopes of having a professional sports career.

It isn't the love of the game that makes some of the best athletes resort to steroids and growth hormones. Star players are not only well compensated by their teams, they're commodities in the ad market. They are offered multimillion dollar contracts to play for a team that expects eventually to get its money back from advertising income, and are paid millions more to advertise products.

This commercialization has altered the ethics of sports and sportsmanship. The cliché that sports builds character has been undermined, and superstar athletes have complained about "having to be" positive role models for young fans. Aspiring superstars know that they can lead less than exemplary lives if they make it and still be media heroes. As celebrities, they are often held to a different standard of accountability for their excesses.

The business of sports has led to many changes. Professional baseball went from a mostly afternoon game to one played primarily in the evening. Football fans have gotten used to many more minutes of commercial time and commentary than minutes of actual play. Football, basketball, and hockey have added breaks to accommodate more television ads. Many sporting events are held in arenas and stadiums that bears a corporate sponsor's name, and these venues are crammed with commercial banners and billboards, real and virtual. Both NASCAR drivers and their vehicles are covered with names and logos. Watching sports broadcasts often means being inundated with commercial messages.

Nutrition, Medicine, and Health

Capitalism and Conscience

To even begin to address the effects that advertising and PR have had on health and on medical practice during my lifetime, I need to clarify some premises, specifically regarding the nature of capitalism. I'm not an anticapitalist or a Marxist, but I do believe in a balance between the virtues of laissez-faire capitalism and those of socialism. I'm not a proponent of Big Government per se, but given a choice between Big Government and Big Business calling the shots, I'll go with the former. However, it doesn't have to be an either/or thing.

Marxism (an innately unworkable notion), socialism, and democracy have a built-in conscience: the collective welfare of the people matters. I know capitalism is an economic system, not a political system, and I'm not saying that capitalists don't have consciences. But it seems to me that being a successful capitalist doesn't necessarily require having a conscience, caring about anyone's welfare but your own, or behaving in a prescribed ethical manner. It often means getting ahead of your competitors by whatever means are available, such as hiring the toxic-waste disposal contractor with the lowest bid and the best propagandists that money can buy.

Capitalism is amoral, and nothing intrinsic to it even attempts to exclude sociopaths from operating and prospering under its rules. Sure, sociopaths can thrive in democracies and socialist states, but if their immoral, unethical, or criminal behaviors are exposed, they can be branded as corrupt, as not being true to their professed principles. This branding doesn't apply to capitalist sociopaths, as they do not need any ethical principles. Under capitalism, the accumulation of capital is an end in itself and, to some capitalists, the end justifies the means.

Contemporary capitalism is embodied in corporate entities whose charter is not to serve the collective good, but to generate profit for owners and shareholders. Advertising and PR campaigns try to persuade us that corporations care about us and are acting responsibly in our best interests, even when that is not the case. These massive advertising campaigns usually have the desired effect on public opinion, or we wouldn't still be bombarded by constant corporate feel-good propaganda. Even the Koch brothers have recently gotten into the act with feel-good ads for Koch Industries, presumably to counter the negative press they've gotten for their self-serving political activism.

A major function of advertising in our society is to provide a persuasive voice for corporations to sell or promote their products or services. Advertisers don't care whether or not you "need" what they're selling, as long as you think you do and buy it. The bottom line in merchandising is pushing product, selling services, moving merchandise—trying to dominate the market.

Food and Drugs

The food industry spends billions persuading us to consume large quantities of foods that adversely affect our long-term health. Then the drug industry promotes pharmaceuticals to counter the ill effects of our unhealthy diets. It's not like the fast-food chains want their customers to die young, but they don't care if consumers overindulge in unhealthy foods, as long as they're getting paid rather than the competition.

If their research reveals that adding even more salt or fat or sugar makes a dish more popular, they'll add it. Your health is not their concern, any more than it's the concern of the tobacco or liquor industries.

When Frito-Lay pushed Lay's potato chips in a campaign that challenged, "Bet you can't eat just one!" it wasn't just hot air; it was a wager backed up by big bucks. If their chips are truly different than those of their competition, it didn't just happen. The food industry has spent a lot of money perfecting snack foods with just the right combination of salt and sugar and fat to stimulate the pleasure centers of the brain in a manner that promotes further consumption. It's known in the industry as the "bliss point."

One of the triumphs of marketing in my lifetime has been the success of bottled water. Perrier started the trend in the United States with a multimillion dollar promotional campaign in 1977 (Hall 2009). If someone had told me in the 1980s that in the next century bottled water would be more expensive than gasoline, I wouldn't have believed him. Bottled water isn't a success because it is uniformly purer or better tasting than the tap water in many localities, but because it's perceived as purer and better tasting. According to the National Resources Defense Council, 54 percent of Americans drink bottled water, 36 percent of them more than once a week, although it costs from hundreds to thousands of times more than tap water (Olson 1999). Much bottled water is just filtered tap water. Certainly, drinking water is healthier than drinking sugary beverages, but tap water would do. There isn't a scintilla of proof that we're healthier due to the change in our water consumption habits.

What's new? Merchants have always been willing to

provide unhealthy pleasures to the masses and to promote them as normal and okay. What's new is having the technological means to refine, amplify, and target methods of mass persuasion in a way that was never possible before. What's new is an army of highly intelligent and effective social engineers using the latest technologies to shape mass behavior in the service of capitalist agendas and goals. Advertising and public relations are highly lucrative professions for their most talented practitioners, whether in the commercial or political arena.

While ad campaigns by the food industry promote unhealthy lifestyle habits, the pharmaceutical industry produces and promotes prescription medications that enable people to treat the symptoms of their unhealthy behavior without changing it. Chronic heartburn? Hypertension? High cholesterol? Keep eating an unhealthy diet, and take this pill.

Americans eat out a lot more often than they used to, as evidenced by the proliferation of chain restaurants and the advertising that supports them. This trend is mass-conditioned behavior. Delicious food is depicted and promoted all day long on TV and in other media, and fast-food chains compete by advertising and supersizing their processed fatty, salty, sugary high-calorie fare. Advertising is a major factor in the current epidemic of obesity, with all its attendant health risks. The treatment of diabetes is a very profitable enterprise for Big Pharma. At the other end of the weight spectrum, we've seen an increase of anorexia and bulimia in young women in our society—a pathological trend largely attributable to advertising. The fashion industry often promotes its products by hiring young, waiflike models, intentionally creating an ideal of slender, youthful beauty that few girls can match but many aspire to. Any perceived flaws are edited out.

Girls grow up comparing themselves to the unattainable ideal they see in fashion magazines and other sources. Many carry this fixation into adulthood and are continuously conditioned by the advertising industry to want to look like professional models and to resist aging. This conditioning can undermine self-esteem at any age and lead to compulsive and unhealthy practices, in pursuit of the ideal image the advertisers present.

Advertisers target children with puffed-grain candy marketed as cereal, processed foods, and kids' meals at fast-food chains that come with a movie tie-in toy you can only get by buying the meal. Ads for children often encourage them to influence their parents' choices. This aggressive merchandising to children is undeniably a factor in the rise of childhood obesity and early-onset diabetes. Kids are an easy target, and many know how to "work" their parents to get what they want. Some advertisers count on this in designing their ads, now that the FCC and the FTC have been largely stripped of their regulatory power over children's advertising.

Pushing Pills

A new lucrative career was created by the pharmaceutical industry: the drug rep. Most of the drug reps I've met were young, attractive, had great social skills and ingratiating demeanors, and had been well trained to promote specific drugs. In the past, advertising for prescription medications mainly appeared in professional medical publications, and drug reps courted prescribers with all kinds of inducements: pens, coffee mugs, calculators, and other trinkets; free meals and resort vacations; "consultant" fees for rating drug company presentations; fees for doing presentations about drug studies that presented the sponsoring company in a favorable light; and other material inducements.

Although I've never been a licensed prescriber, as a mental health professional I've gotten a lot of freebies over the years from drug reps. I've attended presentations and received many a free lunch as well as the kinds of trinkets described above. I regret to say that I didn't manage to snag a Mellaril coffee mug (Mellaril is an antipsychotic drug, no longer widely prescribed due to toxic side effects) with the iconic round, yellow smiley face and the caption "Have a Happy Day"—perhaps the nadir of bad taste in promotional items. But I do have a rubber replica of an item from Freud's antiquities collection. Many are the means of persuasion that drug companies have employed to promote their products.

A major change occurred as product promotions to medical professionals were curtailed, due to new restrictions within medicine, limiting the acceptance of gifts and money from drug companies. Now the pharmaceutical companies market prescription medications directly to consumers, suggesting that their product might be just what you need. Often using the imperative voice, they direct you to discuss their product with your prescriber. A recent issue of *Time* had fourteen and a half pages of ads for pharmaceuticals—almost one-tenth of the magazine.

Of course, ads aimed at the consumer for nonprescription drugs and nostrums have been around for a long time. Some of these ads use the props of medical practice—white lab coats, etc.—to create a positive association or claim scientific validation for the product's efficacy, even when there is no sound scientific body of evidence to back their claims.

The new consumer-targeted ads for prescription medications, which appear in print periodicals as well as on television, generally start out with the theme, "If you have osteoporosis/ erectile dysfunction/allergies/heartburn/COPD/psoriasis/ restless leg syndrome, etc., ask your doctor if this drug is right for you." Then they try to persuade that subset of viewers that has (or thinks it has) the identified malady to try their product, using the usual tricks of the propagandists' trade.

To avoid or minimize subsequent liability lawsuits, the ads often end with a list of possible negative side effects. The overall emphasis is on presenting the product in a favorable light and creating positive associations, while the warnings are often delivered rapidly and in a monotone—the TV equivalent of small print. The risk versus benefit ratio of taking a drug isn't something most viewers are capable of ascertaining, but with the availability of online pharmacies, a discussion with your doctor is no longer a prerequisite for obtaining a drug you're convinced you need.

Drug companies know this and capitalize on it. They spend a lot on research and development, so that they can come up with new patented drugs, for which they can charge whatever the market will bear. They make most of their profits from the sale of new drugs that are perceived to be better than other drugs already on the market. Once the patent runs out and generics are available, the drug no longer generates big profits. A 2008 York University, Toronto, study, "The Cost of Pushing Pills: A New Estimate of Pharmaceutical Promotion Expenditures in the US" (Gagnon and Lexchin 2008), estimates that the pharmaceutical industry spends almost twice as much on product promotion as on research and development.

It's understandable that Big Pharma heavily promotes new drugs that show promise in the market, based on preliminary trials. In my own experience, presentations by medical professionals and drug reps have tended to cherry-pick studies that present their products in a favorable light and overlook those that don't. Even if subsequent research indicates that the new drug is no better than other drugs, strong preliminary sales can generate a lot of profit. As restrictions on advertising and promotional marketing to professionals have changed the marketing landscape, drug companies have tried to eliminate the "middleman" prescriber, pitching their products directly to the consumer.

But the influence of the pharmaceutical industry on medical practice has even deeper roots in the medical community. Only in recent years have board members of medical associations and committees been required to fully disclose drug company affliations and other potential conflicts of interest.

The DSM

I'm not an expert in medicine, but in my clinical practice I've become quite familiar with the Diagnostic and Statistical Manual of the American Psychiatric Association (DSM), and have seen diagnoses come and go over the years. The DSM II was the psychodiagnostic Bible when I started as a mental-health professional, and in that edition homosexuality was listed as a mental illness. Subsequent editions have corrected that error, and each edition attempts to improve the definitions of what is normal and what is pathological, requiring some kind of treatment. The DSM V recently came out, with its new parameters for pathology. Its revised taxonomy will have profound effects on health care expenditures in coming years.

The advertising/PR arm of Big Pharma plays a significant role in the marketing of new drugs for new diagnoses. Has restless leg syndrome (RLS) been an unrecognized medical condition until recently, or was the decision to create the new diagnosis influenced by pharmaceutical companies that can profit by having a new malady to treat? All I know is that when RLS was made an official medical diagnosis, drugs were immediately being advertised to treat this newly identified pathology.

It gets even trickier with psychodiagnosis, because there are usually no biological markers, lab tests, or brain scans that can differentiate between psychiatric diagnoses. The business of diagnostic nomenclature is based on hypotheses that are subject to change. Some people question whether the DSM should be revised by a board comprised of members of a professional association with a vested interest in the number of treatable psychiatric illnesses. The insurance industry tends to have a different perspective on pathology than the APA. A recent study revealed that 69 percent of the APA advisory task force that worked on the DSM V had ties to drug companies (Cosgrove and Krimsky 2012).

ADHD

The controversial diagnosis of attention-deficit/hyperactivity disorder (ADHD) provides an example of the marketing of a diagnosis. I say controversial, not because it's not a valid diagnosis, but because of its overdiagnosis, largely due to Big Pharma's aggressive marketing of amphetamines like Ritalin, Adderall, and Concerta. The reason that stimulants help hyperactive children has been explained as a paradoxical effect. While they make most people speed up, they apparently help some folks with attention deficits to stay focused.

Historically, it's been estimated that something like 5 percent of children have ADHD. But according to an article by Alan Schwarz in the December 15, 2013, *New York Times* article, "The Selling of Attention Deficit Disorder," these days almost 15 percent of children receive the diagnosis by age eighteen. In 1990, approximately 600,000 high school students were taking drugs for ADHD; now there are nearly 3.5 million. The disorder is now the second-most-frequent long-term diagnosis in children, right behind asthma. Sales of ADHD drugs in 2012 were nearly $9 billion, five times what they were a decade earlier.

This explosion in diagnosing ADHD is no accident; it is the result of a two-decade multimedia campaign by pharmaceutical companies, aimed at prescribers, educators, parents, and consumers. Normal child and adolescent behaviors like carelessness, impatience, and forgetfulness have been made pathological in drug company propaganda. The industry exaggerates the benefits and downplays the risks of amphetamine therapy in its advertisements and other promotional efforts, and the FDA has cited the major players for false and misleading claims again and again. In presentations to prescribers, medical doctors hired by manufacturers to pitch their ADHD drugs have provided cherry-picked research findings, portraying the drugs as benign, and downplaying the potential for abuse, habituation, and addiction.

According to Dr. Aaron Kesselheim, a specialist in pharmaceutical ethics Schwarz interviewed, "There are decades of research into how advertising influences doctors' prescribing practices. Even though they'll tell you that they're giving patients unbiased, evidence-based information, in fact they're more likely to tell you what the drug company told them ..."

Beginning in the late 1990s, ads for ADHD drugs in medical journals were supplemented by ads pitched directly to consumers in such periodicals as *People* and *Good Housekeeping*. Parents were told their children's behavior problems could be solved with medication. In an attempt to destigmatize ADHD, historical figures like Socrates, Galileo, Thomas Edison, and Abraham Lincoln were retroactively diagnosed with the disorder. Educators—many of whom liked the idea of an effective medical treatment for disruptive students—passed on brochures provided by drug companies. Shire Pharmaceuticals subsidized the distribution of a comic book in which superheroes explained to children how ADHD drugs could help them.

Despite abundant evidence indicating that perhaps half the children diagnosed won't be impaired by symptoms as adults, manufacturers have distributed promotional materials suggesting that adults with a history of ADHD will need lifelong treatment with pharmaceuticals. Like juvenile ADHD, adult ADHD is overdiagnosed, partly due to drug-industry campaigns that purport to help people identify undiagnosed attention deficits.

The overprescription of amphetamines has led to their abuse by people who don't have attention deficit disorder. They are an underground commodity in high schools, colleges, and universities all over the country. When ADHD medications are taken by people who don't meet the criteria for addiction, they may become habituated to the extra boost they get and unable to imagine facing the day without the amphetamines. Some of these people will be lifelong customers, with or without prescriptions.

A Pill Worth Taking

In my opinion, the federal FDA is a toothless watchdog when it comes to the marketing of purported cures. There don't seem to be any effective laws or regulations to hold advertisers accountable for their claims unless they are outrageously false, for example, "guaranteed to cure cancer." The methodical blurring of the line between scientific fact and unproved assertions has been built into the modern health market.

TV ads for Occuvite, Bausch and Lomb's eye vitamin and mineral supplement state that it can "help protect your eye health" and conclude with the endorsement by an everyman character, who says, "Now that's a pill worth taking!" The Occuvite homepage adds a second phrase, that it "helps replenish vital nutrients your eyes can lose as you age," but both statements are followed by an asterisk. If you hit the "get the facts" button, you read "there are nutrients you can take to help protect your eye health" and that Occuvite "helps replenish vital nutrients to help protect your eye health." But again there are the asterisks, which direct you to the very small print at the bottom of the page: "This statement has not been evaluated by the FDA. This product is not intended to diagnose, treat, cure or prevent any disease."

What is Bausch and Lomb claiming? For whom is Occuvite "a pill worth taking"? Everyone? All senior citizens? A subset of senior citizens who take multivitamins that don't adequately promote eye health? Apparently, the manufacturers have no scientific basis for the claims they make, but they seem to suggest that it can prevent disease, despite the disclaimer. They don't care if you truly need it, only that you buy it because you think you do. That's what advertisers do.

All kinds of cures and purported solutions to health problems are advertised every day on radio and TV and in print and interactive electronic media. Many of them promise results "or your money back," or claim that there's scientific evidence to back their bogus claims. We see ads for nutritional supplements, herbs, aromatic oils, diets, magnets, devices to tone muscles and melt away pounds, fitness routines, "anti-aging" products, fat farms, cures for addiction, self-help books that claim they'll change your life, and other modern analogues of what used to be called snake oil cures.

TV Ads for Medical Services

I remember a time when it was illegal for medical doctors to endorse health products and services or promote their own practices on TV. (The pertinent propaganda technique is *appeal to authority.*) Actors who looked like doctors, with lab coats and stethoscopes, could pitch, but actual physicians could not. Now MDs can promote products or advertise their own services, and hospitals can compete for your health care dollars in the advertising arena. The cost of advertising presumably is added to your bill, as part of the overhead cost of doing business.

On a recent Sunday morning, I watched a half-hour infomercial for the Southeastern Spine Institute. Although it began with an announcement that it was paid promotional programming, it subsequently tried to present itself as one of a series of "medical documentaries," with the title, "The Age of Spinal Medicine." A slick promotional package, it emphasized that the institute was located in Charleston, SC—a popular tourist destination—and that it attracts people from all over the country with neck and back problems. The infomercial claimed that its purpose was "to help educate the community" on advances in spinal medicine, but its clear purpose was to promote the institute.

Slogans like "Get back your life!" and "We're always one step ahead!" were repeated. The viewer was assured about the expertise and competency of the institute's professional staff. Doctors testified that they were using the latest nonsurgical treatments and surgical techniques. All needed services, from diagnosis to surgery to post-op physical therapy, were available "under one roof," and the institute had deals with local hotels in historic Charleston where family members could stay.

The infomercial had the look and feel of a documentary, with people who appeared to be reporters interviewing satisfied customers. Reporters are supposed to strive for objectivity and ask probing questions. These people were actors whose job was to make you think this presentation was a documentary. I feel sure that their questions were scripted. I don't know if the interviewees' answers were scripted or if they were compensated for their endorsements, but there were no surprises in their answers. Nobody had anything but praise for the institute. Some echoed the claim that the treatment had "given me my life back." Several out-of-towners said it had been worthwhile to travel to Charleston for treatment.

The clear purpose of this pseudodocumentary is to convince viewers that the Southeastern Spine Institute is the best option for treatment of spinal problems. While I have no doubt that the institute offers competent services, no objective evidence is presented to show that its treatment is superior to that offered by other institutions. However, the deceptive techniques used to persuade potential consumers is what makes this a "camouflage" advertisement—the TV equivalent of the print advertorial. If you watch it uncritically, you are led to believe that you *know* things, when in fact you only believe them to be true. I wonder how much this series of infomercials cost the institute and how much will be added to patients' bills to pay for them.

As with advertising for legal services, the arms race effect applies. When one medical institution advertises its services, it tilts the playing field in that institution's favor, putting pressure on the competition to advertise too. Advertising does nothing to improve the quality of medical services across the board, but it does add to the cost. Consumers are left to determine whose commercial message is more persuasive when making important decisions about medical care.

Childrearing and Education

We live in a world where, instead of our extended families and communities passing on wisdom or cultural practices to us, we receive homogenized culture from mass media. Family morals and values compete with the media's role models. The role of parents has become diluted by the flood of messages fed to children by corporations that stand to profit from influencing their behavior. By one estimate, advertising aimed at children is a $15–17 billion operation (Shah 2010).

It has been estimated that the average American child is exposed to more than one hundred ads a day, something like forty thousand a year (Media Education Foundation). Children who watch commercial TV are targeted with ads that feature cartoon characters and peer role models who urge them to eat unhealthy food and acquire the latest toys, educating them to be consumer-citizens who want things they don't need. Their ability to influence their parents' buying decisions—the nag factor—is exploited, and their behavior is shaped by the social engineers of commerce. Every Christmas season, parents fight over "must have" toys in stores, not wanting to disappoint children who have come to expect their immediate wishes will be granted. During my lifetime, I've seen the growth of a culture of entitlement, fostered by advertising.

Some children's cartoons are essentially extended advertisements for lines of toys. The stories told may model social values and moral lessons, but in the context of acquiring the toys that will enable children to feel like participants in the franchise. Increasingly, parents have to compete with other role models to shape their children's priorities and choices. I've heard many stories from parents about how their efforts to limit their children's exposure to mass media have been subverted by media-fed peer influences and the ubiquity of commercial messages.

Whole product lines have been created to sell parents on unhealthy food for children. Kraft Foods debuted its line of Lunchables in 1988 and has marketed these kits of processed food with such ad copy as "lunchtime's greatest hits, with more choices of what they love," and "give them more of the stuff they love." The twin marketing strategies were convenience for parents too busy to make lunch for their children and the appeal of tasty but unhealthy lunches for their target market. Lunchables provide children with processed meat and cheese products, crackers and other processed carbohydrates, and in some cases sugary drinks and candy. If kids go to the Lunchables website, they can play games and watch "cool" videos and will be exposed to ads amid the entertainments.

According to *Advertising Age*, Lunchables is "one of the most resilient food brands in America," surviving frequent criticism from health advocates while dominating the kids' packaged-lunch category (Schultz 2014). In 2013 the brand reached $1 billion in retail sales for the first time. Kraft Foods has launched a new line of Lunchable products for teens, called Uploaded, with bigger portions. One of the packages contains deep-dish pizza topped with bacon.

According to a 2007 FTC report on children's exposure to TV advertising, "Food marketing is among the postulated contributors to the rise in obesity rates" (Holt et al. 2007). Parents who try to feed their children healthy diets and teach them to make healthy dietary choices have to compete with the marketing of products that please the palates of young people, but often have high saturated fat, salt, and sugar content. The clear message from manufacturers of junk food is "indulge your children."

Cereal manufacturers produce breakfast candy for kids, and candy manufacturers tell us "candy is delicious food, enjoy some every day." Even if parents restrict their children's intake of unhealthy foods, many kids load up on salt, sugar, and fat anyway, in foods provided by indulgent grandparents, and when they visit friends whose parents aren't as health conscious as their own. Obesity has more than doubled in children and quadrupled in adolescents in the past thirty years; in 2012 more than a third of American children and adolescents were overweight or obese (Centers for Disease Control and Prevention 2014). This epidemic isn't a social accident, but a by-product of social engineering by food marketers.

Even in school, children are exposed to advertising, and their behavior is influenced by marketing schemes. A public school teacher who taught for decades in Virginia told me about one such scheme: If a soft drink manufacturer pays for the scoreboard at the school stadium, not only does it push its product every time someone checks the score, but only that brand of soft drink is sold in the school's vending machines. Other items donated to schools by merchandisers come with similar strings attached, ensuring that students will be exposed to their brand day in and day out. Some school districts get money by allowing advertising in their school buses.

The most dramatic encroachment of advertising into public schools is Channel One, a for-profit "digital content provider" that pitches ads to a captive audience of millions of kids all over the country, since 1990. Participating schools contract with Channel One and receive TVs and VCR/DVD players for classroom use. In return for this audiovisual asset, schools are required to broadcast Channel One's daily ten-minute newscast, including two minutes of commercials. I've never seen one, myself, but my teacher friend confirmed what I've read about the broadcasts: they typically feature "soft news" items. The commercials include promotions for junk food and military recruitment ads.

Raising children has always been a challenge for parents, and we've all heard that it takes a village to get the job done right. Parents need all the help they can get from the community, and for most families, school is a vital part of the village. In my opinion, schools should be ad-free zones, places of education, not commercial indoctrination. But now that more and more schools allow smartphones, children can potentially get pitched every waking hour.

Law and Politics

Law

When I worked in a rural area, I saw a sign on the wall of a small town lawyer's office: "A community too small to afford a lawyer can always afford two." The point of this inside joke seems to be that lawyers profit from conflict and litigation. Now that lawyers can advertise, they hawk their services, promising their prospective clients that they can get them more money than the other guy. The ad market for lawyers has become another arms race, a competition of hyperbolic claims. And, of course, the advertising costs are passed on to the clients.

What was called ambulance chasing in the past has achieved a new kind of respectability, as competing lawyers now claim on TV ads that they'll get you top dollar for your injury. They troll for clients, both for personal-injury claims and class-action suits. While legitimate injury victims certainly may need legal help to get what is due them, fraudulent claims can lead to exorbitant compensation. It seems to me that advertising is complicit in the inflation of health care costs because of such claims.

Effective advertising of legal services doesn't ensure that you have the best representation available, only that you think you do. Some advertisements feature testimonials from clients—"I got $150,000 for my injury!"—while others cite the experience and expertise of the lawyer or law firm.

One local lawyer touts his military service: "He fought for his country, he'll fight for you!"

Some ads invite people who think they've been injured to join class-action suits. But if such suits are successful and millions in damages are awarded, the bulk of the settlement often goes to the law firm. What's left is divided among the individual plaintiffs, none of whom receive much in the way of a settlement. Lawyers don't generally take on class-action suits as a public service. Other ads promise "it won't cost you anything" to see if your claim of injury has merit, without mentioning that you'll pay on the back end. A large percent of any monetary award will be used to pay for your legal representation and for the advertising that attracted you as a client.

Politics

Some special interest ad campaigns try to influence election outcomes and are thus "soft" political endorsements. (One API ad, for example, urges viewers to become "energy voters.") At a more overt level, commercial television has become perhaps the major battleground of the election cycle. Average viewers are so inured to commercial propaganda and the line between fact and opinion has been so thoroughly blurred by professional truth-spinners and propagandists, they are easy marks come election time. According to the *New York Times,* approximately $2.6 billion were spent on political advertisements during the 2008 elections (Seelye 2008). Presidential advertising campaigns now cost hundreds of millions of dollars. An article by Jim Rutenberg in the June 20, 2013, *New York Times Magazine* was titled, "Is Selling a President Any Different than Selling a Pizza?" Mr. Smith isn't going to Washington anymore. He can't afford to run.

Attack ads predominate on radio and TV, using time-tested techniques to make viewers think they're being told the truth. Among these are the grave voiceover, typically freely mixing facts with opinions, and a succession of unflattering images of the person attacked. Sometimes these images are in black and white, in contrast to color images of the candidate who paid for the ad. Such ads are rife with specious premises, misrepresentations, and out-of-context sound bites, all designed to make people feel informed when, in fact, they're being persuaded.

Attack ads have come to dominate the political advertising landscape on commercial television, and it's likely to get worse since the Supreme Court's *Citizens United* ruling that there are no limits on corporate contributions to political campaigns. The social engineers of the propaganda industry know that perception usually trumps facts, and political races often come down to a bare-knuckled brawl between rival propagandists. Knowing that advertising budgets often determine the outcome of political races at the state level, wealthy out-of-state donors are increasing their contributions, changing the face of state politics.

Not all attack propaganda comes in the form of advertising. Some of it comes in the form of informal smear campaigns that systematically spread false allegations and rumors. The belief among conservative Republicans that President Obama wasn't really born on US soil has persisted, despite the proof that he was. This didn't just happen. I believe that the unofficial Republican propaganda machine (with the help of Fox News) has kept repeating the lie and stoking the fires of doubt that it lit. I'm not suggesting that the Democrats don't use propaganda too; I just think the Republicans are better at it.

I don't think I've ever read a more self-congratulatory book than *America's Right Turn: How Conservatives Used New and Alternative Media to Take Power* by Richard A. Viguerie and David Franke. In it, Viguerie (2004, 330) proudly takes credit for the ascendancy of the conservative movement within the Republican Party. He was the first political advertiser/fund-raiser to mount a direct-mail advertising blitz that targeted likely conservatives. By compiling, trading, and selling lists of contributors, he helped unite the National Rifle Association Republicans, the antitax/small government Republicans, the right-to-life/evangelical Republicans, and other factions in a powerful coalition. Viguerie (2004, back cover) has been called the "Funding Father of the Conservative Movement."

Conspicuous by its absence in *America's Right Turn* is any reference to the use of propaganda in any conservative direct-mail campaigns. It's the invisible elephant in the book. The word appears two or three times, but not in the index, although propaganda was an important tool in the conservative takeover of the GOP. I'm not suggesting that only Republicans or conservatives use propaganda, but I've known for decades that it is widely used in their direct-mail campaigns.

I know this because both of my parents were staunch Republicans (my mother still is) and were on a lot of conservative mailing lists. I even got on some, until the advertisers realized that they weren't going to get any money from me. I can't say whether or not the examples I saw were done by Viguerie's advertising agency, but everything I recall reading used propaganda techniques. The mailings didn't use facts and rational reasoning to solicit contributions; they used alarmist language and unsubstantiated assertions, playing on the readers' fears. (Send money, or they'll take away our guns!)

In the 1970s much of the propaganda in the mail was anti-Communist. (Send money, or the Communists will take over!) I remember in particular a newsletter by Fred Schwarz, head of the Christian Anti-Communism Crusade. I was so bothered by the bias and inaccuracies that I actually wrote to Schwarz, asking if we could correspond and discuss some of his unsubstantiated claims. He had the courtesy to write back and decline my invitation, saying that, due to his position in the anti-Communist movement, he didn't have the luxury to engage in dialogue.

America's Right Turn doesn't have formal citations and is propagandistic in tone, throughout. The authors make no pretense of objectivity and, indeed, make no attempt to conceal their contempt for people who might disagree with them. They refer to NPR as "National Pinko Radio." Chapter 6 starts with "Warning: This chapter contains excerpts from liberal media that may be offensive to people with a brain." The book is filled with unsubstantiated assertions such as this one: "Put together all the influential media and you get a score of something like liberals 95, conservatives 5 … That's the sort of monopoly enjoyed by *Pravda* in its Soviet heyday" (Viguerie 2004, 52).

Other propaganda techniques used in the book are distortion, appeal to authority, and glittering generalities. The authors describe the "devastating impact" of direct mail as "like using a water moccasin for a watchdog—very quiet and very effective" (Viguerie 2004, 136). If I taught a college course in propaganda, I'd use this book as a teaching text.

Direct-mail political propaganda is still around. My mother was recently so alarmed by an anti-Obama mailing that I had to talk her down. The letter featured "quotes" attributed to the president that were anti-American and pro-Arab fabrications. All my mother needed was a dose of objective reality to calm her down. I asked her, "Do you *really* think Obama could have said those things in public speeches during his first term [as the letter alleged] and have been elected to a second term?" She thought it over and realized that she'd been lied to.

Civil disagreements between political rivals seem to be a thing of the past. Regardless of which candidate wins, professional propagandists as well as TV and radio stations are the guaranteed winners in this new equation of mass persuasion. The rest of us lose.

We lose because we have to rely on slogans, sound bites, and attack ads to make our decisions in the voting booth, instead of reasonable discussions of issues and candidates' qualifications for office. We lose because candidates have to raise a lot of money to pay for advertising campaigns. Politicians have to engage in fundraising from the day of their election or reelection until the end of the next election. We lose because in a mud-slinging contest, everyone gets muddy.

Religion and Spirituality

Advertising Faith

A widespread advertising campaign some years ago featured billboards with purported "signed" messages from

God. Some of them were: "We need to talk." "One nation under me." "Life is short. Eternity isn't." "Don't make me come down there." "You think it's hot here?" and "Big Bang Theory? You've got to be kidding." In a dark twist on the billboards from God campaign, someone sponsored a billboard with the message, "Your pretty face is going to hell—Satan."

God wants you to go to church, or so Christian advertisers would have you believe. Denominational leaders say it doesn't matter where you go to church, as long as you go somewhere, but churches and denominations compete for market share, and crossovers are always welcome. (It's called transfer growth.) Every televised church service is an advertisement for that church, and a recent TV ad for a local church had the pastor saying, "We're excited about what God is doing at [our church]!" as if God had singled out his church for exciting things that you wouldn't want to miss. The highest steeple in town is a kind of advertisement in itself, as is the cathedral-sized megachurch.

Much religious advertising meets the criteria for propaganda. Believers claim knowledge—for example, "I know that my Redeemer liveth"—which nonbelievers would classify as beliefs, because no objective proof exists for such a proposition. I respect the faith of my Christian brethren, but faith isn't fact. Some readers may not see it this way, but from my viewpoint many faith-based statements meet the definition of the propaganda technique of assertion—that is, stating opinion as fact. As Brian Anse Patrick puts it, religion and propaganda "thrive in much the same soil" (Patrick 2012, 189). The first usage of the term propaganda was in the Roman Catholic Church, where it referred to a committee of cardinals that oversaw matters related to the propagation of the faith.

A good example of an assertion-based religious message is a quarter-page advertisement that appeared in the *State* newspaper, promoting a talk by a Christian Science speaker: "How Christian Science Heals Bodies and Restore [*sic*] Lives." The ad copy states, "Healing isn't a random miracle, but a natural result of God's Law of Love." That may make sense to a believer, but it means nothing specific to me. (I've certainly never thought of healing as a random miracle.) Christian Science is described in the ad as "a system of Christian healing."

Due to the commercial promotion of Christianity in general and the marketing activities of individual churches, ministries, and megachurches, there are Christian advertising agencies, marketing consultants, retailing associations, dating services, publishing houses and bookstores, a booksellers association, rock concert promoters, "technologies for worship" conferences, radio stations, and at least one television network. Some megachurches publish directories of Christian-run businesses, for those who want to spend their money within the faith community. An online website for Kingdom Ventures touts itself as "a different kind of venture capital firm [where] we believe that God is at work in the venture capital and private equity industry ..."

In his book *Shopping for God: How Christianity Went from in Your Heart to in Your Face*, James B. Twitchell (2007, 1) asks "What happens when there is a free market in religious products, more commonly called beliefs?" He writes about "religion dealers" and the competitive market for customers, whether they're called believers, parishioners, members, or seekers. He writes that people attend church to experience individual and group sensations, such as the sense of being forgiven or "saved."

Religious advertising is nothing new. In 1908 a Presbyterian minister, Reverend Charles Stelzle, published *Principles of Successful Church Advertising*. A major turning point on the road to today's religious marketplace occurred in the 1950s—the advent of signs with movable letters, which were placed in front of church buildings. These signs contain information about church services or activities, or sayings intended to promote attendance. The sayings and quotes can be fairly generic ("get right with God"), promote the doctrinal beliefs of the church ("once saved, always saved"), threaten eternal damnation for nonbelievers ("Repent! Jesus is coming soon!"), or feature clever recruiting slogans ("What's missing from CH__CH? UR"). I suspect many Christians don't think of these signs in front of the church as advertisements, but they are. Now many churches have big digital signs that serve the same function.

According to Twitchell (2007, 24), in 1900 there were 330 different religious groups in the United States, and now there are more than two thousand. The traditional Protestant denominations (Lutherans, Methodists, Episcopalians and some Baptist denominations) have been steadily losing market share to nondenominational churches, megachurches, and evangelical congregations. The fastest-growing segment consists of Pentecostal and charismatic churches. Trying to regain ground, the United Methodist Church has spent millions on its Igniting Ministry campaign, whose slogan is, "Open minds. Open hearts. Open doors." Other traditional denominations have also launched ad campaigns.

Megachurches, Crusades, and Televangelists

Megachurches—also known as big box churches or McChurches—are churches with a regular weekly attendance greater than two thousand. There were approximately ten in 1970; by 1990 there were over 250 (Twitchell 2007, 229). Twitchell (2007, 227) describes the megachurch as "a new kind of delivery system, a much more efficient experience of what we go to church for: communal and individual sensation." The typical megachurch does not have an altar or crucifixes. Instead of a sanctuary, there's an auditorium; instead of a pulpit, there's a performance space for the pastor—who often reads from a teleprompter—and other performers.

Megachurches with names like Faithworld and New Life Church stage performance extravaganzas with rock-concert trappings: dropdown Jumbotron screens, studio-quality sound systems and electronic synthesizers, strobes and stage lighting, and even smoke machines and laser light shows. Of course such extravaganzas require stage hands, control booths, and sound engineers. Some megachurches have mobile cameras and camera crews to capture the rapture and run it live on the Jumbotron screens, magnifying the effect of the congregation's fervor. This is not your father's church. Megachurches usually have a campus outside the auditorium and provide services throughout the week, from child care to fitness classes to counseling services. Some have restaurants and gift shops.

Before there were televangelists and megachurches, there was "America's pastor," Billy Graham, arguably Protestant Christianity's most successful promoter. He staged giant rallies, borrowing from traditional tent revivals, concluding with an "altar call" for people to come forward and be saved. According to the Billy Graham Evangelistic Association, his so-called crusades (talk about aggressive marketing!) and fifty years of a radio broadcast called *The Hour of Decision* have led millions to accept Jesus as their savior. Some of his crusades were televised, virtual advertisements for evangelical Christianity.

Televangelists who have become household names include Oral Roberts, Jim and Tammy Bakker, Jimmy Swaggart, Pat Robertson, and Jerry Falwell. In 2007 there were more than 150 syndicated evangelical programs on AM radio, and Christian broadcasters controlled more than 10 percent of US broadcast licenses (Twitchell 2007, 11). Gospel and Christian rock stations may as well be advertising with every song they send out on the airwaves.

Obviously, some megachurch pastors and televangelists are quite wealthy, unapologetically so. Getting rich from religion is certainly nothing new, and there continue to be evangelists and churches that assure their congregations God wants them to be rich.

The Spirituality Marketplace

I've focused so far on Protestant Christian advertising and marketing, without going into the Roman Catholic Church's long history of propagandistic self-promotion and its deceptive public relations campaigns when its own sins and failures are revealed. Suffice it to say for the purposes of this book, neither the Catholics nor the Orthodox Church have advertised as much or as conspicuously as the Protestants. Certainly non-Christian True Believers also advertise and run public relations campaigns; it's just not as "in your face" as the activities of the Christian majority in the United States. I haven't been exposed to any Muslim, Jewish, or Hindu advertisements or PR campaigns that I can recall.

That having been said, there are many non-Christians with spiritual beliefs. They constitute distinct submarkets, and almost anything is up for sale in the spirituality market. Check online or in New Age magazines and you'll see promotional messages for everything from Anusara yoga to Zen massage, packaged as spiritual practices or services. New Age and neo-pagan groups abound. The Church of Scientology offers courses that can show you how to become a "Scientology Clear." Its promotional materials don't promise anything like salvation, but suggest that achieving the state of Clear means your personal performance will be enhanced, because you will no longer have a "reactive mind" holding you back.

Inner Traditions, a mail-order company, offers books representing a wide range of spiritual and religious traditions and practices. Many of the books are about purported health-related practices, but others promise to share ancient spiritual secrets, reveal mysteries, and even teach you about Druid sexual practices. Yet others will teach you Buddhist breathing, Tai Chi techniques for discharging chi energy, and Taoist cosmic healing.

Comfortably packaged faith is a commodity on the open market, and many religious institutions are always looking for ways to swell the ranks of their faithful followers. Although some true believers may find it unseemly to advertise God, others argue that God moves in mysterious ways, and that the end—saving souls—justifies the means.

Popular Culture

Early in the twentieth century, American society was transformed by advertising and public relations. As Edward Bernays and his colleagues used Freudian psychodynamics and propaganda techniques to create and stimulate new appetites in the public, the United States changed from a needs-based economy to a desire-based economy. This shift was reflected in a speech by President Herbert Hoover to an audience of advertisers, where he said, "You have transformed people into constantly moving happiness machines that have become the key to economic progress" (famousquotes.com).

As I was growing up in the 1950s and 1960s, certain themes emerged that seem in retrospect an antecedent to what we now call memes: ideas that self-replicated and spread like viruses, becoming a part of the culture as a result of their daily exposure in mass media. We'd entered a period of post-war prosperity and as a society, we were open to whatever we perceived as progress. Part of this trend resulted from advertising in the popular media, especially the new kid on the block, TV. I now see it as the beginning of popular culture being fed to us from the top down, rather than arising from grass roots and spreading organically in society.

The themes and notions that took root in post-WWII American culture included "dress for success," "keeping up with the Joneses," "life in suburbia," "bigger is better" (with its corollary, "if one is good, two is better"), new labor-saving devices for the housewife, and the whole cult of "modernity." Modernity meant having the newest and the best—at least as good as the Joneses—and getting a new car every two or three years to demonstrate that you were a success. Ads in magazines and on TV offered status symbols for sale, and professional career success, we were told, was contingent on keeping up with fashion. Even in high school, you had to dress like the in crowd if you wanted to join the in crowd.

The fashion industry couldn't exist without advertising.

At the low end, it invites people to express their individual styles by choosing from among trendy lines of off-the-rack clothing. At the high end, fashion can be an expensive hobby or obsession or a competition for status among the very rich ("Who are you wearing this season?"). Oscar Wilde famously said, "Fashion is a form of ugliness so intolerable that we have to alter it every six months."

Mine was the first generation of children in modern society to be recognized as a distinct and profitable market, to be catered to and shaped as consumers. It started with such things as coonskin caps, popularized by the Disney TV show *Davy Crockett*, and caught fire with such products as Barbie dolls for girls and Red Ryder BB guns for boys. Syndicated afterschool shows like *Superman* and the *Mickey Mouse Club* proved that there was a vast youth market waiting to be exploited. (I was the first kid on my block to order a cheesy Superman suit, from an ad in the back of a comic book.) The success of Elvis Presley and later The Beatles on the *Ed Sullivan Show* indicated that rock 'n' roll was here to stay and that teens were a rich vein to be mined.

The advertising and public relations industries have subsequently had decades to study the markets and hone their tactics, as consumers became habituated to TV and its techniques of mass influence. When the Internet came along, influence peddlers had all the techniques they needed to exploit that medium too. We media consumers, conditioned as we are, constitute a captive audience for pop-culture marketers.

Who is responsible for taking Christ out of Christmas? The secularization and commercialization of the holiday is almost entirely due to the advertising industry and its exploitation of the season as a marketing opportunity. Because of advertising, Valentine's Day, Easter, Halloween, and Thanksgiving aren't just days on the calendar but marketing seasons.

Because popular culture no longer arises from the grass roots, we now live more and more in a world monoculture. Distinct cultural norms are homogenized as we all feed from the same media outlets and are exposed to the same role models. As older generations die out, dialects and traditions are lost and are replaced with generic successors. Whole cultural "root systems" are being severed by the engines of progress.

Women from so-called primitive tribes in the Amazon basin have been conditioned to believe that they can't be beautiful without cosmetics. From Katmandu to Cape Town, the uniform of jeans and printed tees is ubiquitous. The Disney empire has established Magic Kingdoms in Paris, Tokyo, and Hong Kong. People in developing countries who can't afford to eat at KFC and McDonalds envy those that can and aspire to join their ranks. We all watch the same movies, with ever-more familiar action heroes and superheroes.

None of this is accidental. Commercial social engineering is no longer culture bound; it is an international enterprise, controlled by the international corporate state. There are still original artists in all nations and cultures, but increasingly their cultural contributions are eclipsed by the most hyped, the most popular, the superstars and the winners of shows that promote "idols" and "divas," and celebrities du jour. This brave new world is the result of advertising, marketing, and public relations campaigns.

The Environment

Advertising and public relations play a significant role in the growing climate change crisis in a number of ways. They promote the endless consumption of many things nobody really needs, whose production exploits natural resources that could be used more wisely. The petroleum industry spends millions of dollars annually to assure us that we can trust it to be responsible; that our current reliance on fossil fuels is not a significant cause of climate change; and that there is no urgent need to develop sustainable, renewable energy resources. Daily feel-good ads on TV encourage us to trust the energy giants, whatever they do.

Additional millions are spent by the natural gas industry to convince us that natural gas is the fuel of the future and the key to America's energy independence and prosperity in the twenty-first century. While it may cause less pollution than petroleum, it's still a fossil fuel and a part of the problem, not the solution. According to a *USA Today* article by Wendy Koch (2013), natural gas will replace coal as the largest source of US electricity by 2035. Thanks to "advanced technologies," natural-gas production is projected to grow steadily, at least through 2040.

Just because there hasn't been a major contamination of groundwater due to fracking thus far doesn't mean that it can't happen in the future, as use of the technology is expanded. And if an aquifer were to become contaminated with natural gas and lubricating chemicals, it would likely be an irreversible ecological catastrophe, affecting all plants and animals that depend on its water. Large areas could become permanently uninhabitable.

In their advertising and public relations campaigns, the

petroleum and natural gas industries refer to hydraulic fracturing and other new "unconventional" extraction processes as "safe and proven," as if there were absolute guarantees they would never result in catastrophe. If the energy industry has its way, thousands of new wells will be drilled all over the country, wherever sufficient oil shale is found to justify the costs of drilling. In fact, nobody knows the long-term effects of pumping millions of gallons of chemically treated water deep under the earth's surface, because hydraulic fracturing is a relatively new technology.

The industry propaganda emphasizes that the chemically treated water is pumped far deeper than the aquifers and talks about layers of concrete and steel that protect underground water from the natural gas being extracted. But we're talking about a process that pulverizes rock deep underground. No industrial process I'm aware of is without risks. We have the ability to penetrate deep, fracture rock, and extract natural gas, but we don't have the technology to restore or to make repairs deep underground or to permanently seal leaks.

The more we frack, the more chances there are that an accident may occur due to human error. And even barring accidents, can we expect barriers of concrete and steel to withstand a major earthquake, without rupturing and injecting natural gas and massive amounts of chemicals into the water supply? In my opinion, anyone who claims to know that fracking is "safe and proven" is lying.

There has been a substantial increase in earthquakes (so far, only minor) in some areas in Oklahoma and other states where there is a lot of fracking. Seismologists can only speculate at this point about the link between fracking and increased seismic activity. I believe that we're dealing with forces of nature science doesn't yet fully understand, for the short-term profitability of exploiting "unconventional" extraction techniques.

The vast majority of climate scientists agree that our reliance on fossil fuels is implicated in global climate change and that if we don't cut down on carbon emissions we're heading for global catastrophe, perhaps even an extinction event. The energy industry appears to be deep in denial, focused on the short-term benefits of extracting and burning fossil fuels and the profitability of the enterprise.

The worst case scenario is that the escalation of global warming will continue until we reach the point where the biosphere can no longer sustain life. Future generations, facing extinction, may curse us for our shortsightedness and greed. And commercial propaganda, a major force in our history of industrial growth and our modern consumer society, will have played a major role in the death of the biosphere.

Conclusion

In his book *The One-Dimensional Man,* Herbert Marcuse (1964, 10) asks, "Can one really distinguish between the mass media as instrument of information and entertainment, and as agents of manipulation and indoctrination?" I certainly can't. The media teat we all feed from informs, amuses, and attempts to define and shape us. Advertising and PR are two of the most influential tools of centralized social engineering, and Edward Bernays was quite accurate when he described the cognoscenti of the new, modern social science of influence as an "invisible government."

What can we do about a propaganda industry that tries to condition us to be constantly moving happiness machines, always in need of more goods and services? What can we do to help keep our children and their children from becoming homogenized consumers, cogs in the juggernaut of commerce? How can we remain mentally healthy in an environment polluted with infotoxins?

The only antidote to infotoxicity is education.

The ideal goal of public education would be to provide all students not only with the basics—literacy, numeracy, history, tech skills, science and the humanities—but with knowledge of the mechanics of thinking and the choices we have as independent thinkers. Unfortunately, the invisible government doesn't want an education system that turns out independent thinkers. They want conditioned consumers and like things fine the way they are. Free thinkers are as hard to herd as cats, and they have a tendency to want to look behind the curtain.

In an ideal democracy, children would be inoculated against propaganda and media manipulation because they would learn about the techniques of mass persuasion, starting in middle school. Any high school graduate would be able to readily identify which propaganda techniques or heuristics have been used in a message or campaign. The ranks of professional propagandists would shrink, because it would be difficult for them to keep their influence invisible. With this kind of public education and a truth-in-advertising law with teeth, information eventually would replace propaganda in advertising. But it's not going to happen unless the public sees the danger we face from infotoxicity, and demands change.

The goal of the short-lived (1937–42) Institute for Propaganda Analysis (IPA) was to inoculate the public against the insidious influence of propaganda by teaching people "how to think rather than what to think." Clearly, there were those with a vested interest in propaganda who didn't want the institute to carry out its campaign of public education. Some suggested that it would only lead to unhealthy public skepticism, rather than the stated goals of encouraging rational, independent, and well-informed public discussion of important issues.

The social scientists, historians, educators and journalists who made up the IPA distributed flyers, bulletins, and books identifying the most common propaganda techniques. Their materials were disseminated to high schools, colleges, and civic groups. When the institute suspended operations in 1942, lack of funding was cited as the reason. However, it's possible the real reason was that it could have undermined US propaganda operations during WWII.

Alas, although the IPA's initial prewar educational efforts had met with some success, it wasn't revived in the postwar era. Part of the reason we're a propaganda society today is that we don't have anything like the IPA to educate the public at large, and propaganda analysis isn't widely taught in our public schools. And that's the way the advertising and PR industries want it.

During my career I became a practitioner of cognitive behavioral therapy (CBT). I told clients and colleagues that if I had a gospel to preach, it was rational thinking. There are different approaches to CBT, and what one school of practice calls "thinking errors," another calls "irrational self-talk." But they all share the core concept that our reactions to the things that happen to us are determined largely by what we think and tell ourselves. We can choose to reframe the meanings of trivial and important events in our lives, to minimize our suffering, and maximize the effectiveness of our responses to whatever comes our way.

Does losing at something you really wanted to accomplish make you a loser? Will you never get over your heartbreak, or is that just a self-fulfilling prophesy? Does your self-esteem depend on getting that promotion at work? Do you really need this thing or that, or do you just really, really want it? Do other people have the power to make you angry, or do you generate your own anger in response to what others do or don't do? Could rejection by a lover drive you to suicide?

The principles of CBT correlate to the Buddha's teaching that all suffering arises from attachments and to the wisdom of the Serenity Prayer (whether or not you start it with "God grant me …"). As I've said to many therapy clients, you don't have to be in recovery from substance abuse to carry the Serenity Prayer in your back pocket. It is a way of quickly differentiating what you can change and what you can't, and adjusting your attitude accordingly.

We all have thoughts that are rational and thoughts that are irrational. In my experience, most people have trouble telling their irrational thoughts (often characterized by shoulds, musts, and "always" and "never") from their rational ones. Advertisers capitalize on our irrational thinking and the behaviors it engenders. Rational thinking is a learnable skill, and practicing it for over three decades has spared me a lot of unnecessary pain. That's why I've tried to pass it on to loved ones and in my practice as a therapist.

Not only do I wish that the ABCs of propaganda analysis were routinely taught in English and social science classes in our public schools, I wish rational thinking was part of the core curriculum, from elementary school through high school. Training in rational thinking is the opposite of indoctrination; it truly teaches one how to think, not what to think—the stated goal of the Institute for Propaganda Analysis. I don't share Walter Lippmann and Edward Bernays's notion that the masses in a democracy are a herd that has to be led by an elite class of social engineers. I think that people can be conditioned to behave like herd animals if they're treated like herd animals or liberated from the yoke through education.

Who could argue with the assertion that we need critical, independent thinkers to advance as communities, nations, and a planet? We call it thinking outside the box, and to some degree it's a learnable skill set. It's in our long-term best interests as a nation and a species to teach rational thinking to as many as we can reach. However, this radical proposal runs counter to the corporate culture behind the invisible government, and its short-term goals of profitability and accumulation of maximum wealth. Conditioned consumers are easier to influence than independent thinkers.

The corporate state is doing its best to indoctrinate us. In his "Redemption Song," Bob Marley exhorted us all to liberate ourselves from the invisible shackles of what he called the Babylon System:

> Emancipate yourself from mental slavery
> none but ourselves can free our minds.

But each of us who sees and understands the motives and the media mechanics of mass persuasion and its toll on the soul can help raise the consciousness of others. Education is highly contagious, when it gives people things they can use.

It can inoculate people against indoctrination. We could all use more signal and less noise.

As I've made clear, I believe that our propaganda society threatens American democracy. I also believe that the propaganda industry keeps us endlessly acquisitive, and overreliant on fossil fuels. I can only hope that we'll wake up and learn to rely on renewable energy resources in time to avert a global climate change catastrophe.

As a therapist, all one can do to help others is plant seeds. If they're healthy seeds in receptive soil, some will take root and grow.

As a psychologist, a US citizen, and a citizen of the world, I'm alarmed by the hold that propaganda has on the average person, throughout the industrialized world and beyond. I wrote this book to plant seeds, because I think we're at a critical crossroads in the history of American democracy. It's my hope that some of the seeds herein will take root and generate public dialogue about of the role of advertising and public relations in our lives.

Appendix 1: On Commodities

"Don't you know that if people could bottle the air, they would? Don't you know that there would be an American Air-Bottling Association? And don't you know that they would allow thousands and millions to die if they could not afford to pay for air? I am not blaming anybody. I am just telling how it is."
—Robert Ingersoll

"Things are in the saddle and ride mankind."
—Ralph Waldo Emerson

"Beware the naked person who offers you clothing."
—African proverb

"Give that man a Dewey button" used to be a joke that meant someone deserved a worthless reward. Most people had expected Dewey to win the presidency in 1948, and when he lost to Truman, his campaign button immediately became synonymous with worthlessness. Today a genuine Dewey button for sale on eBay might be worth something to someone, but only what some collector is willing to pay for it.

What is the worth of a minor Picasso sketch? A sequined jacket worn by Elvis in Vegas? A picture of a celebrity doing something scandalous? The endorsement of a product by Madonna? A first edition of *Gone With the Wind*? A baseball autographed by Willie Mays? An Oscar that belonged to a dead movie star?

What is the worth of your own visage, your story, your pain, your grief?

Everything Is a Commodity

Everything has become a commodity. In a world where pizza and cable have replaced bread and circuses, everything is potentially marketable—not just land, tools, shelter, food, and services but relationships, inside knowledge, contrived experiences, popular tunes, and reputations—even fame, or infamy, itself. All these are on the open market, at today's price.

For a fee you can chat with your psychic friend or a sex hotline worker on the phone, get financial advice from alleged experts, get a makeover, gratify your child's conditioned desire for the toy of the month, go to a theme park and pretend you're having an adventure, meet with a prominent politician, or even change your appearance—because your body is a commodity too.

John Wayne Bobbitt discovered that he could market his reattached penis in the porn industry. Oliver North parlayed his lies to Congress into a career in talk radio and television. Marilyn Manson learned that it pays to think up new ways to shock and disturb parents.

The songs you grew up with were commodities even then, but now you hear the notes reproduced with soulless precision in elevators, edited versions of the chorus in TV ads for pharmaceuticals. Good Ol' Charlie Brown sells you insurance, and Bugs Bunny sells you high-speed cable service for your PC.

The engine of commerce has co-opted our memories and thoroughly permeated our mental environment with messages telling us what we need. The process moves a lot of plastic through the market.

Form over Substance

Sales pitches and shopping environments, designed with Pavlovian precision, form associations that put us in a mind-set to buy. To marketers who design catalogues and shopping environments, the customer is the commodity. Most people will tell you that slick, expensive advertising campaigns do not determine their choices as consumers, but companies wouldn't pay for advertising if it didn't demonstrably increase sales.

In the realm of advertising and marketing, form trumps substance. Things don't have to be real, as long as the consumer buys into the illusion. Years ago, on a visit to Hilton Head Island, my wife and I saw billboards advertising a gift shop named Jamaican Me Crazy. We'd just returned from two years of living in Jamaica and decided to check the place out. While the shop had a Caribbean ambiance and offered brightly colored, tropical-themed gifts, there was nothing from Jamaica for sale. The background music wasn't even Jamaican; it was Trinidadian calypso, not reggae. I am sure the shop owner didn't care that he or she was selling only the concept of a Jamaican shopping experience, while not selling any real Jamaican merchandise.

Similarly, the term *Zen* has been appropriated to promote a variety of products and services that have absolutely nothing to do with Zen Buddhism. While nobody would think to call their massage parlor Baptist Massage, some entrepreneurs have staked a claim to Zen Massage. The term *hip* refers to a state of knowledge or awareness, as in "hip to what's goin' down." "I'm hip" originally meant "I understand," not "I'm cool." Hipness isn't a quality that imbues fashions or material things or activities any more than Zen does. But that hasn't stopped advertisers from selling the notion that things can be hip, and that you can be hip if you buy them. Whatever sells.

Mass Influence

The principles of the relatively new science of psychology have been applied more systematically to influence mass behavior nowhere other than the advertising industry. As surely as Gutenberg made public opinion possible with his invention of movable type, the marriage of mass communications technology and applied psychology reached a whole new level of effectiveness during the world wars. Some of the giants of the postwar advertising industry graduated from this school of propaganda.

Pavlov showed that a neutral stimulus like a bell can stimulate food-related physiological reactions. A predictable response becomes linked with a previously irrelevant stimulus. Every advertising professional understands this principle, which is why pretty women in bikinis are draped on the hoods of vehicles in ads. Whether or not you believe that you are influenced, cleavage sells cars.

Everything is for sale in the postmodern market economy—not only the latest must-have products but anything that effectively associates a given product with something that consumers want: an imagined experience, a familiar and desired feeling, an association with fame or success, a stroked ego, or a stoked prejudice. We can buy the transient illusion of comfort or love or acceptance or attractiveness or rectitude or forgiveness, if we have the money to pay for it. Hucksters even peddle God's love on infomercials.

The marketing of divine intercessions is nothing new, of course. The Catholic Church sold pardons and indulgences for centuries. But now anyone with the trappings of a religious vocation and the money to buy ads can hawk God's favor. Pieces of the True Cross are still available if you call in the next ten minutes.

And if you're not religious, there are plenty of people who will try to sell you a piece of magic. Just go to the Disney store at your local mall, or order it online.

Money and Magic

Throughout most of history, wealth has resided in land, livestock, precious stones and metals, tools (weapons or means of production), and progeny. Wealth has now been reduced to an abstraction called money, which takes form as metal, paper, plastic, and electronic binary series stored in computers.

The means by which a mint-issued, colored, printed piece of paper is assigned worth in the market is indistinguishable from magic. It is worth precisely what its recipient thinks it is worth. The only difference between a so-called hard currency and soft currency is belief.

Every day the worth of a dollar (or a drachma, pound, or

ruble) fluctuates in value relative to other currencies, based on what the international market believes it to be worth on that day. A worthless counterfeit bill accrues the face value when someone accepts it, believing it to be real money.

Who can doubt that if Picasso had eaten a lavish meal at a restaurant, then drawn a quick doodle and the words "Five Hundred Picasso Francs" on a napkin and given it to the waiter, that the management would have accepted it as payment, and even given him the change? They would do so knowing that the napkin would henceforth be worth at least five hundred francs. Why? Magic.

Aleister Crowley defined magic simply as "the science and art of causing change to occur in conformity with will" (Crowley 1929–30, xii). In his 1962 essay, "Hazards of Prophecy," Arthur C. Clarke famously said that any sufficiently advanced technology is indistinguishable from magic. I submit that if a thousand people see a self-proclaimed magician levitate, and others subsequently pay good money to see him repeat the feat, this qualifies as an act of magic. Whether or not he ever leaves the ground is irrelevant, because people respond according to their beliefs at least as often as they do to their knowledge. A product is worth exactly what people are willing to pay for it.

Going back to the thought experiment about Picasso: if you buy the premise, there are several explanations for why his napkin would suddenly become a marketable product. The most obvious explanation has to do with the role of fame as a commodity. Another factor is the perceived scarcity of the product. (If Picasso had executed only one "Five Hundred Picasso Francs" napkin, it would be worth considerably more than if he had tossed them off routinely.) Some have suggested that certain people such as Picasso, by virtue of their artistic genius, are authentic magicians, because they can change the way in which people look at things.

What Is It Worth?

What is the worth of a sequined jacket worn by Elvis in Vegas? Filter in the fame factor and the scarcity factor, and the answer is: a lot more than it cost Elvis. But how much depends entirely on what people *think* it is worth.

How does this differ from what can be described as magical thinking, when we discuss (for instance) the animistic beliefs of "primitive" people? No universal standard exists for establishing the value of a commodity, and we all rely on the modern alchemists of wealth to tell us the value of transmuted lead in today's market.

What is the worth of a photo of a celebrity committing a scandalous sexual act? That depends whether we're talking about Rob Lowe or Pee Wee Herman. Homemade porn films of Pamela Anderson, one imagines, are worth more than those of Tanya Harding. The fame factor dictates what the image is worth, based on how hot a commodity the celebrity is. It also determines the worth of a commercial endorsement by a celebrity such as Madonna.

A first edition of *Gone With the Wind* or a baseball autographed by Willie Mays is bound to continue to accrue value with each passing year and with each sale. Through an act of associative magic, the fame factor dictates the price for an Oscar that was awarded to a deceased movie star, although it is identical to every other Oscar. Artifacts that once belonged to a major celebrity are bound to go up in value after the person's death.

What Is Your Worth?

What is the worth of your visage, your likeness? Unless you're already famous, or resemble a famous person, it's probably relatively worthless in today's market. But if you have the look that fashion experts say is in this year, win an Olympic gold medal in the right sport, or suddenly achieve fame because of something you did, marketers will pay for the right to associate your name and face with their products. Images of certain dead celebrities remain commodities, which marketers can exploit if they pay the estates the going rate in the market. Through the technological miracles of computer animation, images of John Wayne and Marilyn Monroe can even continue to perform new roles for the camera, and generate new profits.

What is your life story worth? If you perform some extraordinary feat, your first-person account may become a commodity that you can financially exploit, although many others also may profit from telling your story in the third person. If you achieve a certain degree of name recognition because of a terrible misfortune or misdeed, your story may become grist for the media mill, with or without your consent. We can all tune in at 11:00 p.m. for the full story, and advertisers will pay for our attention.

Pain and loss also frequently get assigned a dollar value in the market. But how much your pain or your grief is worth depends largely on the quality of your legal representation and on the judgments of a jury. Even deaths resulting from accidents and catastrophes that nobody could have foreseen or prevented often send families and their attorneys on a frenzied search for a culprit with deep pockets. Someone with lots of money has to be at fault; someone has to pay. Grandpa was not responsible for the fifty years of heavy smoking that gave him lung cancer. Phillip Morris made him do it.

Social Engineers

Many individuals promoting innovations have been blamed by their critics for trying to be social engineers, for trying to shape mass behavior in accord with their own agendas, without having been given the authority to do so by the people. But with the rise of the corporate state, the culture is being shaped to an alarming degree by a tiny oligarchy of rich businessmen who happen to own the mass media. They are the real social engineers. They claim they only provide us with the things we tell them, via our purchases, we want. But did we really ask for a throwaway culture of conformity, an unending menu of trendy trivial pursuits, and homogenized, dumbed-down news coverage—a culture driven by ever more pervasive advertising?

We have been systematically conditioned to think we need and deserve the unnecessary commodities and instant gratifications provided by mega-merchants and media moguls and to accept the attendant limitations on true choice. In this brave new world we are now more consumers than true citizens, and we continue to sell our democratic birthright for instant access to pizza and cable.

In the early days of radio and television, broadcasters used to say that the airwaves belong to the people. If that were ever true, it ended when the regulations were changed to remove any control over the ratio between programming content and advertising. And with that change, the line between the two began to blur even more. Merchandising seems to have become the primary function of the mass media.

Television Formats

During the seven years I lived in Austria (1958–62) and Germany (1970–73), I watched little television, but saw a whole different approach to advertising than I was used to stateside. Advertising came in extended blocks of perhaps ten or fifteen minutes, and those ads paid for the programs that followed. The programming was not broken up into half-hour and hour-long programs underwritten by advertisers who competed to place their ads in the shows with the best ratings for that month. The offerings varied from week to week, and one show might last seventeen minutes, another an hour and thirty-seven minutes. The length and content of programs was not driven by advertising.

Until broadcasters changed their rules, networks and stations had to offer at least X minutes of programming for every Y minutes of advertising. We used to see about twenty-five minutes of programming and five minutes of ads per half hour. The abolition of the ratio of programming to advertising not only opened the door to infomercials and rerun movies being interrupted every six minutes by ads, it eventually resulted in the current standard of roughly forty-five minutes of program content per hour of broadcasting. And because the cost of advertising is assessed according to a program's current or recent ratings, program quality has long been secondary to popularity. Except in the case of a few perennial "public interest" programs that continue to run due to the prestige they bring a network news division, advertising revenues usually determine what shows survive and what shows are cancelled.

At different levels of the market, television programs are commodities, ads are promoting commodities, and we—the

Nielsen-rated consumers of television programming—are commodities sold by the numbers to advertisers. The result is endless imitation in program planning, formula scripts written in N-minute segments, and programming aimed at the lowest common denominator. We didn't ask for this; we have been systematically conditioned to accept it. And then, adding insult to injury, we're told we chose it. Card sharks and sleight-of-hand magicians have a name for this trick of forcing a card on someone: Hobson's Choice.

Corporate Censorship

Certain messages aren't tolerated by the advertising/merchandising establishment that runs television, even if one can pay the going rate. The people who own the airwaves don't have to air anything they think might upset the corporate applecart, as Kalle Lasn pointed out in his book, *Culture Jam*.

When Lasn's Media Foundation tried to buy time on broadcast and cable networks for "subvertisements" that provoke consumers to think about their buying choices, they were turned down by almost everyone (Lasn 1999, 30–32). The corporate state doesn't like its North American citizen-consumers being reminded of the gluttony of energy and natural resources that we have come to enjoy and to take for granted. Such memories might have a chilling effect on commerce. Our conditioned avarice has become a meta-commodity on the world market.

Mass perceptions are up for sale, whether or not they reflect reality. From time to time the nuclear and coal industries have put out cute little propaganda cartoon ads depicting simple solutions to the problems created by our ever-increasing appetite for energy. The ads, like so many others, are designed not to inform, but rather to evoke positive feelings and create positive associations.

More Media Manipulations

Gullibility is defined by the market. Even youth is packaged as a commodity. Untold millions of dollars have been spent on Botox and on so-called "anti-aging" creams and lotions, as if we had really found the fabled fountain of youth. The ads don't claim that the products temporarily reduce certain signs of aging; the merchandisers truly want us to believe the fiction that their products can reverse the aging process.

Advertisers program us to wear what they tell us is cool or "in," as if conformity of dress were a social virtue. They even tell us we can buy hipness, the antithesis of trendiness, with the purchase of khaki pants, because Jack Kerouac wore them. It doesn't matter to the bottler whether his water is purer or better tasting than what you get from your tap, only that you believe it is. Evian is naive spelled backward.

Trust

Commodities are, by their very nature, exploited; and you are a commodity on the free market. This brings me to the penultimate commodity I'll discuss here: trust.

Everyone with something to sell, from the snake-oil salesman to the investment adviser, has the same theme implicit in his pitch: trust me. Because perceptions can be more powerful forces in the market than facts, trust itself is a commodity for sale on the open market. There's a whole industry of public relations advisors and spin doctors who effectively practice the psychology of mass persuasion.

Trust me. The whole point of accountancy as a profession

is accountability: you can trust these numbers. But an audit is only as accurate as the accountant is trustworthy. The Andersen accounting firm appears to have been complicit in the book cooking at Enron. Its product, trust, made the firm a lot of money as long as it maintained an image of trustworthiness, but Andersen is no longer in business.

In a larger sense, the Enron debacle was a reminder of the emperor's manifest nakedness. Apparently, nobody in the financial community, except for those who profited, noticed that these major corporations had built palaces out of paper, because a respected accounting firm told us we could trust them. Ooga booga! Magic.

How much should we trust the advice of investment experts and the system they assure us is still respectably, even splendidly, clad? Who can believe that only the companies currently under investigation have exploited our trust and cashed in on our ignorance? Perception, not reality, determines the worth of a commodity traded on the stock market.

Selling Security and Fulfillment

The last commodity I'll cover here is the feeling of security, which is peddled by everyone from investment brokers to insurance salespersons to cults and salvation merchants. Security is the illusion of being in control.

There's an almost universal fear of losing control—of our minds, our behavior, our health, our wealth, our lives. Death is the ultimate source of insecurity for most of us, since none of us know what is on the other side of that inevitable door, somewhere in our futures. Freud said that fear of death is the beginning of slavery. There are organizations and whole industries that take advantage of this existential fear. Their goal is to make us feel secure.

Security is an idea, a feeling, not a fact. Most people in the modern world are only a paycheck (or four or ten) from homelessness and destitution. No matter how carefully we manage our portfolios and invest for our retirements, none of us is truly secure. Most intelligent, informed people in the middle class know, at least in the back of their minds, that a national or worldwide economic depression could wipe us all out. The pundits assure us that nothing like the Great Depression could ever happen again ("trust us"), but some of our fellow citizens feel secure only because they have gold and guns stored up, in case the unthinkable happens and civilization as we know it collapses.

Whether we put our faith in the free market, government, gold bullion, a divine plan, or guns and ammunition, none of us is truly safe from the slings and arrows of outrageous fortune. Those of us who know and accept that to be alive is to be inherently vulnerable have a kind of freedom relative to those who don't.

I believe that there's a universal longing, and that what we all ultimately seek is priceless—not for sale anywhere—although many of us try to fill the void with things. We are conditioned by society to settle for what is available here and now, and that conditioning establishes the rules for the majority. No matter the name attached to the object of desire—fame, success, wealth, sex, power—there are people out there who will sell it to you.

Have We Already Lost Our Birthright?

Kalle Lasn wrote in *Culture Jam* (1999, xv) that the flip side of cool is cynicism. The same corporate megalith that sells us cool cars and fashions and opinions has silenced most people who think, *There's something very wrong with this picture*. They say, "That's just the way things are. You can't fight City Hall. What could I possibly do about the emperor's naked greed?"

I suspect that the corporate oligarchy believes it has already won the hearts and minds of the masses in the Western industrialized world, and that within another generation or two, resistance against the corporate state will be literally unthinkable. But the systematic corporate takeover of the institutions of democracy during the last century has led to consequences we are only starting to see, not only in the demonstrations that have become fixtures at the world financial summits, but in the Occupy and similar anticorporate movements in many industrialized nations.

It seems to me that the US government, for example, is now a partially owned—some would say wholly owned—subsidiary of the corporate state. Buckminster Fuller characterized the international corporate oligarchy as LAWCAP: capitalism shaped by lawyers for its own perceived benefit. He coined a collective term for the leaders/social engineers of LAWCAP: "a Grunch of Giants." They make the robber barons of antiquity look like small-time operators.

Saving Democracy

If it's true that our system of government is now only a simulacrum of true democracy, can anything be done to reclaim our democratic heritage? Or is it too late to revive a government truly "of, by, and for the people?"

In *The Strawberry Statement* James Kunin (1970, 74) wrote, "One too many persons has been educated, and one too many wires has linked people's thoughts together, for power to breed power anymore." This was written in the 1960s and can be easily dismissed as hippie-era idealism. But perhaps the Internet will prove to be the last bastion of democracy, uniting people around the world in its defense, and eventually validating Kunin's hopeful prediction.

For all their wisdom, the founders of our country could not possibly have foreseen the Industrial Revolution or the power of the mass media to shape collective behavior. They could not have envisioned corporate entities that have all the rights of citizens, including the right of free speech, which has allowed the corporate oligarchy to bombard us with whatever propaganda it thinks will serve its own interests. They did their best to establish a government amenable to the collective will of the people, a government that can be reshaped by amendments to the Constitution. Freedom isn't a commodity on the open market, but a right. It can be stolen by the rich and powerful, but not permanently, if the spirit that shaped this nation still lives.

Appendix 2: 100 Things You Learn on TV

Whenever we watch commercial TV, we're addressed by an array of voices. The voices speak to us, en masse, as individuals. We may be addressed with easy familiarity, with a confidential tone, or in the imperative voice. The voices may joke with us, or cajole. Some entertain, some inform, some attempt to influence or persuade us. George Orwell's predictions in *1984* about the use of doublespeak and doublethink are validated by commercial broadcast media. Many commercials seem to take place in alternative universes that resemble our own. There is such a barrage of facts, opinions stated as facts, half-truths, admonitions, suggestions, misrepresentations, and Alice in Wonderland logic. The softening of language and logic is no by-product of commerce; it's part of a strategy, something the late underground cartoonist Vaughn Bode labeled "masstasizing." (Look up his classic strip *The Rudolf* online at Junkwaffel.com/archives to see this brilliant mordant satire for yourself.)

What follows is a list of things I've copied down verbatim over the years as I've watched broadcast TV, things stated as if they were facts and that stood out as examples of doublespeak and doublethink, meaningless phrases that seem to mean something, or outright social conditioning. The techniques used include metaphor, advice, admonition, paradox, "weasel wording," hyperbole, oxymoron, flattery, cliché, and reverse cliché. I present my list in a random sequence for the most part, but the reader might enjoy organizing the items by category and looking for techniques or patterns.

1. Most people will never tell you if you have denture odor.
2. Peace of mind can be bought (Safeco Insurance).
3. Softness means freshness (Sunbeam bread).
4. Anyone can be beautiful (modeling agency).
5. Candy is delicious food. Enjoy some every day.
6. Soap can bring you back to life.
7. A fragrance can make you beautiful.
8. You can never be too thin or too rich.
9. There is no such thing as too much romance.
10. Wearing footpads is like having a new pair of feet (Dr. Scholl's).
11. Coke is the biggest taste you've ever found.
12. Cologne drives women crazy, and perfume makes you irresistible.
13. Coffee gives you serenity and vitality.
14. Flowers say what words can't.
15. While you're asleep, the other half of the world is awake.
16. Roman Meal invented whole-grain goodness.
17. A greeting card is a little bit of yourself.
18. Finding no spots on your glasses is a moment of glory.

19. When you find your flashlight, it hardly ever works (battery ad).
20. You owe it to the one you love to use Close-up.
21. Revco has everything you don't think they have.
22. Weird Harold will pay you to buy a car from him.
23. Your banker can give you security with no ifs.
24. Tic-Tac-Dough is everybody's favorite game of strategy, knowledge, and fun (TV game show).
25. It's amazing the way you feel every time you eat Yoplait.
26. Clint Eastwood *is* Dirty Harry.
27. You can get a complete library of the world's greatest music for $12.95.
28. There's word that can stop the hurt: Anusol.
29. You have bad breath more than you think.
30. Something can taste expensive (Meisterbrau).
31. You'll live longer if you sleep on a Beautyrest mattress.
32. You'll never get the Oldsmobile Calais out of your mind.
33. Naturally, every dog wants fresher breath (Milkbone).
34. The Jedda isn't a car. (It's a Volkswagen.)
35. Totally improved Pampers make babies 100 percent drier and happier.
36. Something can be "outrageously" creamy (Yoplait).
37. Drugs can work hard or even harder.
38. A car can be intelligent (Saab).
39. Saabs are alive. (A 1991 ad said your Saab will give its life for you.)
40. You can wash away a day of aging every day (Olay Beauty Cleanser).
41. Not all wonder drugs work wonders. (Bayer, the wonder drug that works wonders.)
42. A Carnival cruise is more fun than anything.

43. There's more for your life at Sears.
44. You're splendid. (Vanderbilt allows you to discover "the splendor of you.")
45. Taste can be quantified. (Riunite Spumante has more taste than champagne.)
46. Coffee should please all the senses (Nescafe).
47. No matter how you treat your feet, Dr. Scholl's make you feel like dancing.
48. You can taste the truth (Diet Pepsi).
49. You *can* have it all (Cadillac).
50. You *can* go home again.
51. At Doscher's, you get better.
52. No one deserves a better deal than you do.
53. *Time* magazine brings you closer to living.
54. Oil of Olay is the one secret fifty million women share.
55. Honda lawnmowers are easy to start, or else … they're not?
56. Kraft mayonnaise is blended more than three thousand times.
57. There is such a thing as an anti-aging cream (Frances Denny).
58. They always have what you're looking for at Affordables.
59. You want every day to be your best (*Esquire*).
60. Rice Krispies is tops in complex carbohydrates.
61. Stayfree pads absorb all of your worries.
62. You can plug in to thirty-day freshness (room deodorizer).
63. A piece of Wrigley's spearmint gum puts a sparkle in your eye and a spring in your step.
64. With a name like Smuckers, it has to be good.
65. Ants and roaches deserve to die (Black Flag).
66. Nothing feels as good as Grape Nuts.

67. Now you can have your cheese and eat it too.
68. Bugs have a science of surviving.
69. The Salad Shooter fits anywhere.
70. Vanish Drop-Ins make your toilet sing (though not necessarily well).
71. Nothing makes you feel as good as fine jewelry (Service Merchandise).
72. Something happened to real food, you know, the kind that tastes real good (beef ad).
73. Mazda is intensely committed to your total satisfaction.
74. Nobody does as much as Maalox Plus.
75. Kellogg's and cornflakes are inseparable.
76. There's nothing basic about Basic Fruit.
77. Grey Poupon is so fine, it's made with wine.
78. You have to get excited about something, so why not Kellogg's Corn Flakes?
79. Dogs don't know that Purina Beggin' Strips aren't bacon.
80. Carnival cruises cost a lot less than you think.
81. It took Louis Rich to make turkey so right.
82. Your food will never taste its best until you sprinkle it with Accent.
83. You can search all over the universe and not find a better deal than at Charleston Autoplex.
84. Never let them see you sweat.
85. Your mattress is a battleground of thwarted desires. (Sleep Number Mattresses).
86. There's nothing mellow about Mellow Yellow.
87. Speed Stick deodorant gives 110 percent.
88. Lady Speed Stick protects you like a man but treats you like a woman.
89. Everybody needs a Yugo sometime.

90. Eating Kellogg's Corn Flakes is like having a party in your mouth.
91. If a kid looks good, he feels good (back-to-school ad).
92. You can't be a kid without Jell-O pudding.
93. Neosynephrine provides relief in a nanosecond.
94. GMAC is the official sponsor of America's dreams.
95. Nobody can save you more money than Jeep Eagle.
96. The Best of Old Time Piano is sure to make your party the happiest time ever.
97. Reeboks let U.B.U.
98. Michelin makes the tires you need.
99. Doctors know there's a flaw in eggs (Eggbeaters).
100. Too much of a good thing is a good thing (Mercury Marquis).

Bibliography

Bernays, Edward. (1923) 2011. *Crystallizing Public Opinion*. New York: Boni and Liveright. Reprint, Brooklyn: Ig Publishing. Citations refer to the Ig Publishing edition.

———. (1928) 2004. *Propaganda*. New York: Horace Liveright. Reprint, Brooklyn: Ig Publishing. Citations refer to the Ig Publishing edition.

Centers for Disease Control and Prevention. 2014. "Childhood Obesity Facts." August 13. www.cdc.gov/HealthyYouth/obesity/facts.htm.

Cialdini, Robert. 1984. *Influence: The New Psychology of Modern Persuasion*. New York: Quill.

Classic All-Star Commercials. 2013. DVD. San Diego, CA: Legend Films.

Cole, Robert. 1998. *The Encyclopedia of Propaganda*, vol. 2. New York: M. E. Sharpe, Inc.

Cosgrove, Lisa, and Sheldon Krimsky. 2012. "A Comparison of DSM-IV and DSM-5 Panel Members' Financial Associations with Industry: A Pernicious Problem Persists." *PLoSMed* 9, no. 3; doi: 10.1371/journal.pmed.1001190.

Creel, George. 1920. *How We Advertised America*. New York: Harper.

Crowley, Aleister. 1929–30. *Magick in Theory and Practice*. New York: Castle Books.

Deitz, Corey. "What are the top ten radio formats?" About.com. Accessed December 10, 2014. http://radio.about.com/cs/funradiothings/f/faqradio6.htm.

Famous Quotes. 2011. "Herbert Hoover Quotes." www.famousquotes.com/author/herbert-hoover.

Floyd, A. J. 2013. "A citizens guide to understanding corporate media propaganda techniques." *Internet Post,* October 17. http://theinternetpost.net/2013/10/17/a-citizens-guide-to-understanding-corporate-media-propaganda-techniques/.

Gagnon M-A., and J. Lexchin. 2008. "The Cost of Pushing Pills: A New Estimate of Pharmaceutical Promotion Expenditures in the United States." *PLoS Med* 5 no. 1: doi:10.1371/journal.pmed.0050001.

Geary, James. 2011. *I Is an Other: The Secret Life of Metaphor and How It Shapes the Way We See the World*. New York: Harper Collins.

Hall, Noah. 2009. "A brief history of bottled water in America," *Great Lakes Law* (March 26). http://www.greatlakeslaw.org/blog/2009/03/a-brief-history-of-bottled-water-in-america.html.

Holt, Debra J., Pauline M. Ippolito, Debra M. Desrochers, and Christopher R. Kelley. 2007. "Children's Exposure to Television Advertising in 1977 and 2004: Information for the Obesity Debate: A Bureau of Economics Staff Report." Federal Trade Commission. http://www.ftc.gov/reports/childrens-exposure-television-advertising-1977-2004-information-obesity-debate-bureau.

Information Clearing House. "Language: A Key Mechanism of Control: Newt Gingrich's 1996 GOPAC memo." Accessed November 16, 2014. www.informationclearinghouse.info/article4443.htm.

Koch, Wendy. 2013. "U.S. forecasts natural gas boom through 2040." *USA Today,* December 16.

Kornberger, Martin. 2010. *Brand Society*. Cambridge: Cambridge University Press.

Kunin, James Simon. 1970. *The Strawberry Statement*. New York: Avon Books.

Lasn, Kalle. 1999. *Culture Jam: The Uncooling of America*. New York: William Morrow and Company.

Lepore, Jill. 2012. "The Lie Factory: How Politics Became a Business." *New Yorker,* September 24.

Lippmann, Walter. (1922) 1997. *Public Opinion*. Reprint, New York: Free Press Paperbacks.

Luntz, Frank. 2013. "Why Republicans Should Watch Their Language." *Washington Post,* January 11.

Marcuse, Herbert. (1964) 2002. *One Dimensional Man: Studies in the Ideology of Advanced Industrial Society*. Reprint, London and New York: Routledge.

Media Education Foundation. 2005. "Advertising: Exposure and Industry Statistics." www.mediaed.org/Handouts/AdvertisingExposure.pdf.

Media Reform Information Center. "Links and Resources on Media Reform." Accessed November 16, 2014. www.corporations.org/media.

Morin, Monte. 2014. "Smoking Remains Global Growth Industry." *Los Angeles Times,* January 9.

Olson, Erik D. 1999. "Bottled Water: Pure Drink or Pure Hype?" National Resources Defense Council, April. www.nrdc.org/water/drinking/bw/chap2.asp.

Orwell, George. (1949) 1956. *The Orwell Reader*. Reprint, New York: Harcourt, Brace and Co.

Packard, Vance. (1957) 1980. The Hidden Persuaders. Reprint, Brooklyn: Ig Publishing.

Pasquale, Frank. 2014. "The Dark Market for Personal Data." *New York Times,* October 17.

Patrick, Brian Anse. 2012. *The Ten Commandments of Propaganda*. London: Arktos.

Pratkanis, Anthony, and Elliot Aronson. (1992) 2001. *Age of Propaganda: The Everyday Use and Abuse of Persuasion*. New York: Henry Holt and Company.

Quoteswave. "Adlai Stevenson II Quotes." Accessed November 16, 2014. www.quoteswave.com/textquotes/96113.

Rutenberg, Jim. 2013. "Is Selling a President Any Different than Selling a Pizza?" *New York Times Magazine,* June 20.

Schultz, E. J. 2014. "Lunchables Targets Lucrative Teen Market," *Advertising Age,* May 19. http://adage.com/article/news/lunchables-targets-lucrative-teen-market/293263/.

Schwarz, Alan. 2013. "The Selling of Attention Deficit Disorder." *New York Times,* December 15.

Seelye, Katharine Q. 2008. "About 2.6 Billion Spent on Political Ads in 2008." *New York Times,* December 2.

Shah, Anup. 2010. "Children Are Big Business." *Global Issues,* November 10. www.globalissues.org/article/237/children-as-consumers#.

Smokin': Classic Cigarette Commercials. 2011. DVD. Sherman Oaks, CA: S'more Entertainment.

Stelzle, Charles. 1908. *Principles of Successful Church Advertising.* New York: Fleming H. Revell Co.

Twitchell, James B. 2007. *Shopping for God: How Christianity Went From in Your Heart to in Your Face.* New York: Simon and Schuster.

Tye, Larry. 1998. *The Father of Spin: Edward L. Bernays and the Birth of Public Relations.* New York: Henry Holt and Company.

Vicary, James. 1950. "How Psychiatric Methods Can Be Applied to Marketing Research." *Printers' Ink.*

Viguerie, Richard A., and David Franke. 2004. *America's Right Turn: How Conservatives Used New and Alternative Media to Take Power.* Chicago: Bonus Books.

Williams, Armstrong. 2014. "The Exploitation of College Athletes." Townhall.com, April 9.

Wolken, Dan. "North Carolina probe: Advisers steered athletes to bogus classes." *USA Today,* October 23.

Index

R

U

V

W

Y

Z